T0055060

The Treaty of Versailles: A Very Short Introduction

VERY SHORT INTRODUCTIONS are for anyone wanting a stimulating and accessible way into a new subject. They are written by experts, and have been translated into more than 45 different languages.

The series began in 1995, and now covers a wide variety of topics in every discipline. The VSI library currently contains over 550 volumes—a Very Short Introduction to everything from Psychology and Philosophy of Science to American History and Relativity—and continues to grow in every subject area.

Very Short Introductions available now:

WAVES Mike Goldsmith
WEATHER Storm Dunlop
THE WELFARE STATE David Garland
WILLIAM SHAKESPEARE
    Stanley Wells
WITCHCRAFT Malcolm Gaskill
WITTGENSTEIN A. C. Grayling
WORK Stephen Fineman

WORLD MUSIC Philip Bohlman
THE WORLD TRADE
    ORGANIZATION
    Amrita Narlikar
WORLD WAR II Gerhard L. Weinberg
WRITING AND SCRIPT
    Andrew Robinson
ZIONISM Michael Stanislawski

Available soon:

VOLCANOES Michael J. Branney and
    Jan Zalasiewicz
METHODISM William J. Abraham
C. S. LEWIS James Como

MATHEMATICAL FINANCE
    Mark H. A. Davis
REPTILES
    T. S. Kemp

For more information visit our web site

www.oup.com/vsi/

Michael S. Neiberg

THE TREATY OF VERSAILLES

A Very Short Introduction

OXFORD
UNIVERSITY PRESS

Oxford University Press is a department of the University of Oxford.
It furthers the University's objective of excellence in research, scholarship,
and education by publishing worldwide. Oxford is a registered trade mark of
Oxford University Press in the UK and certain other countries.

Published in the United States of America by Oxford University Press
198 Madison Avenue, New York, NY 10016, United States of America.

Library of Congress Cataloging-in-Publication Data
Names: Neiberg, Michael S., author.
Title: The Treaty of Versailles : a very short introduction /
Michael S. Neiberg.
Description: Oxford [UK] ; New York, NY : Oxford University Press, 2019. |
Series: Very short introductions | Includes bibliographical
references and index.
Identifiers: LCCN 2018035687| ISBN 9780190644987 (pbk. : alk. paper) |
ISBN 9780190645007 (epub) | ISBN 9780190645014 (online component)
Subjects: LCSH: Treaty of Versailles (1919 June 28) | World War,
1914-1918—Peace—History.
Classification: LCC KZ186.2 .N455 2019 | DDC 940.3/141—dc23
LC record available at https://lccn.loc.gov/2018035687

1 3 5 7 9 8 6 4 2

Printed in Great Britain
by Ashford Colour Press Ltd., Gosport, Hants.
on acid-free paper

Dedicated to the memory of Jeffrey Grey

Contents

List of illustrations

Preface

The process of peacemaking lasted longer than the First World War it endeavored to end. The Paris Peace Conference began on January 18, 1919, on the anniversary of the coronation of the German emperor Wilhelm I in the Palace of Versailles in 1871. That event had occurred at the end of the Franco-Prussian War, which had resulted in the unification of Germany and the seizure by the new Germany of two formerly French provinces, Alsace and Lorraine. Although the anger in France over these events had largely dissipated outside of right-wing circles by 1914, the First World War reawakened the memory of the harsh terms that Germany had imposed on France half a century earlier. Those terms had included not just the loss of territory but also an occupation and a large financial indemnity, which the French paid ahead of schedule. Opening the Paris Peace Conference on such a historic anniversary served to remind the French of why, ostensibly, they had fought the war and who would pay for the damages this time. It has also contributed to the image of the Paris Peace Conference as one motivated primarily by vengeance.

Although the senior statesmen stopped working personally on the conference in June 1919, the formal peace process did not really end until July 1923, when the Treaty of Lausanne was signed by France, Britain, Italy, Japan, Greece, and Romania with the new Republic of Turkey. Lausanne was a renegotiation prompted by the failures of the one-sided Treaty of Sèvres, signed in August 1920 but immediately rejected by Turkish forces loyal to the war hero Mustafa Kemal. Sèvres had partitioned Turkey, ceding much of its territory to Armenia, Greece, France, and Britain, with Italy receiving a large zone of influence in southern Anatolia. The sultan had approved the treaty, but Kemal then led an army that deposed the sultan, threatened a renewal of war in the Middle East, and forced a true negotiation at Lausanne.

The conference also produced the Treaty of St. Germain with Austria in September 1919, the Treaty of Neuilly with Bulgaria in November 1919, and the Treaty of Trianon with Hungary in June 1920. These treaties meted out relatively lenient terms to Austria, especially given the Austrian elite's central role in starting the war in 1914. Hungary came out much worse than Austria did, largely to punish Hungarians for their postwar flirtation with a communist movement. Thus the conference had as much to do with postwar politics as perceptions of prewar guilt.

But the centerpiece of the Paris Peace Conference was always the Treaty of Versailles, signed on June 28, 1919, five years to the day after a teenaged Serbian nationalist, Gavrilo Princip, had assassinated Austrian archduke Franz Ferdinand and his wife in Sarajevo. The treaty and the conference are thus closely linked but not quite synonymous. None of the other treaties bear such a heavy historical responsibility for the world they created or the conflicts that followed, although perhaps they should. The Treaty of Sèvres in particular created the conditions for massive change in Turkey, Central Asia, and the Middle East. Still, it is the Treaty of Versailles for which the Paris Peace Conference will probably be best remembered, and most often damned.

The dozens of statesmen, diplomats, and advisors who assembled in Paris in 1919 have come in for heavy criticism for writing treaties that failed to give Europe a lasting peace. Even many of the people most deeply involved with the peace process recognized their shortcomings early on, in some cases before the text had even been drafted. Perhaps most famously, British economist John Maynard Keynes wrote a scathing indictment of the treaty in a 1920 bestseller entitled *The Economic Consequences of the Peace*. He predicted that the economic arrangements of the peace treaty would destabilize the European and global economies, leading to major financial crises. Similarly, American president Herbert Hoover criticized the Treaty of Versailles in his memoirs for causing the worldwide economic depression that began in 1929.

Participants quickly grew disillusioned by the old-fashioned horse trading and back-room dealing that overwhelmed the ideals and principles of those who had hoped to fashion a better world out of the ashes of the war. Few people came out of Paris optimistic about the future. Woodrow Wilson's senior advisor on the Middle East, Columbia University professor William L. Westermann, captured the views of many participants in his final diary entry from Paris, which described the treaty as "wrong in spirit and quite wrong in its methods." Time soon proved him right. It is a great tragedy that so many people like Westermann had come to Paris optimistic only to leave totally disillusioned.

The Germans had hoped until the very end for a moderate treaty based on negotiation or the idealistic principles of Woodrow Wilson. Wilson's ideas, as articulated in his Fourteen Points speech of January 1918, included a League of Nations, an end to secret diplomacy, freedom of the seas, and a reduction of national armaments. He also hoped to reshape the borders of Europe to remove nationalism as a cause of international conflict. Wilson saw his Fourteen Points as the basis for the construction of a new world order. Critics saw him as hopelessly naive about the true inner workings of the world. On seeing the Fourteen Points, French prime minister Georges Clemenceau quipped that God himself was content to give mankind just ten. More importantly, the British saw Wilson's program as a threat to their own power in the postwar world. Simply put, there was no point in fighting so hard to win the war if victory came on Wilson's terms.

The Germans, however, had believed in the Fourteen Points because they offered a glimmer of hope. Germany therefore reacted with fury and anger to the final terms of the treaty. The Allies searched for German officials who would affix their names to such a lopsided treaty, then summarily called them into the majestic Hall of Mirrors at Versailles for a short and anticlimactic signing ceremony. The Germans were not the only ones who were disappointed. French marshal Ferdinand Foch, the man who had done as much as anyone to secure Allied victory on the battlefield over those same Germans, protested the treaty by declining to attend the signing ceremony. Foch believed that the treaty did not do enough to ensure French and European security from a resurgent German threat. The Chinese delegation, too, stayed away in order to protest the cession of economic privileges in the Shandong Peninsula to Japan. Several senior Allied officials either resigned in protest at the terms of the treaty or strongly protested portions of it. Some saw the treaty as too harsh toward Germany, others as too lenient. Almost everyone agreed, however, that the great challenge of the postwar years would be to find ways to rebuild Europe on the basis of a flawed treaty.

On the historical and legal side, the treaties that came out of the Paris Peace Conference were no more harsh than the Treaty of Frankfurt that had ended the Franco-Prussian War. They were in fact much more lenient than the treaties Germany imposed on Russia and Romania in 1918. The Treaty of Brest-Litovsk, signed in March, took away Poland, Finland, the Baltic states, Ukraine, and Belarus from Russia. With those territories went almost one-third of the Russian population and arable land, as well as half of its industrial enterprises and a crippling 89 percent of its coal output. Shortly thereafter, the Germans imposed the Treaty of Bucharest on Romania, forcing the Romanians to lease their oil wells to Germany for ninety years and to give the Carpathian Mountain region to Austria-Hungary and the Dobruja to Bulgaria. Both treaties put German puppet governments in place.

The Treaty of Versailles justifiably annulled the harsh terms of both Brest-Litovsk and Bucharest. It also proceeded from less acquisitive principles than those that had motivated the Germans. Defenders of French and British policy claimed (correctly) that had Germany won, its leaders had planned to impose treaties on the model of Brest-Litovsk and Bucharest on the British and French. In other words, they claimed, the Treaty of Versailles was far more reasonable than any peace that would have resulted from a German victory. Nor did the treaty demand an Allied victory parade through Berlin or the long-term occupation of any portion of Germany until the Germans had paid the indemnity in full. The Germans had imposed both conditions on the French in 1871.

To make flattering comparisons with such harsh treaties is, of course, to damn with faint praise. Other defenses of the treaty might note the relative stability of the 1920s as evidence of a reasonable foundation for rebuilding that the treaty left to Europe. French diplomat Aristide Briand and his German counterpart Gustav Stresemann negotiated the Locarno Treaty in 1925, which led to German admittance into the League of Nations. It earned the two men the 1926 Nobel Peace Prize. Locarno left a legacy that led to the Kellogg-Briand Pact, which renounced war as a means of resolving international disputes; Germany's signature on the pact produced great optimism across Europe. It also helped to make possible the 1929 Young Plan that renegotiated German war debt and reduced the reparations that the Treaty of Versailles imposed to a manageable level. Had the international economy not collapsed soon thereafter, there could have been further acts of reconciliation. In other words, it is not too much to put the blame for the crises of the 1930s on the Great Depression more than on the Treaty of Versailles itself.

The Treaty of Versailles also left Germany in a surprisingly strong geostrategic position. By creating Poland, Czechoslovakia, and the Baltic states, the treaty put buffer states between Germany and one of its traditional rivals, Russia. Fighting among the new states weakened them, and the geography of their new borders made them difficult to defend. Thus Germany emerged from the war with small, relatively weak states on its eastern border. By making both Germany and the Soviet Union pariah states, moreover, the Allies inadvertently opened the door to cooperation between them. For example, it enabled the Treaty of Rapallo, signed in 1922, which buried all grievances the two had against one another and allowed Germany to test new military equipment in Russia, far away from prying French eyes. It also gave each state an incentive to see Poland as a mutual enemy, especially since the Allies had created Poland largely out of formerly German and Russian territory. German nationalists called Poland "the bastard child of Versailles," and Soviet diplomats often referred to it as "Western Belarus" in order to deny it even a nominal place in the new Europe.

To a lesser extent, the same might be said of the German relationship with Italy. Although a nominal victor in the war, Italy, too, came away deeply dissatisfied with the treaty. Like the Germans, the interwar Italian government railed against the perfidy of the French and the British. This shared anger helped to lay a foundation for German-Italian cooperation after the war. Finally, because most of Germany's overseas colonies had been costly to operate in the years before the war, their loss enabled the Germans to focus resources on Europe. In other words, Germany managed to emerge from the Treaty of Versailles in a position that gave it plenty of opportunities if it could rebuild its economy and play its cards skillfully.

Serious German and French strategists read the treaty this way, arguing that it had left France in a far weaker position in 1919 than it had been in 1914. In particular, France no longer had an alliance with Russia to balance Germany, and intense French efforts to build Poland into a reliable eastern ally proved hard to sustain. Nor had Allied politicians taken Foch's advice to detach the German lands west of the Rhine River and create a separate Rhenish state tied to France by a mutual security pact. Instead, the treaty compromised by demilitarizing the Rhineland and imposing limits on the size of the German army and the kinds of weapons the Germans could possess. As Foch predicted, however, these limits proved almost impossible to monitor and the Germans found ways to skirt them, such as the Rapallo agreements to train soldiers and test equipment in Russia.

Points in its defense notwithstanding, it is difficult to contradict the views of contemporaries and later scholars who have seen the treaty as a great missed opportunity and a source of considerable anger and disillusion in Europe and around the world. When in 1945 the leaders of the United States, the Soviet Union, and Great Britain gathered in Potsdam to end the Second World War, they all blamed the failures of the Treaty of Versailles for having made the war of 1939–45 necessary. The final decisions reached at Potsdam in 1945 were deeply influenced by these memories and the desire on the part of almost everyone at Potsdam to atone for the mistakes of their predecessors a generation earlier.

Of course, we must accept the basic truth that no document, even if thoughtfully written and elegantly implemented, could have closed the Pandora's box that Europe opened in 1914. No treaty could have explained to the Germans why they had lost or made them accept the basic fact of their defeat. Instead, having been lied to by their senior leaders, millions of Germans accepted the convenient fiction that their armies had not really been defeated on the battlefield but had instead been betrayed at home. The fact that Allied armies never invaded German soil helped to fuel that poisonous myth, which German politicians intentionally spread to serve their own purposes. By June 1919, that version of history was already commonplace in Germany, and not only in right-wing circles.

Nor were the Allies, desperate to reduce defense expenses and the risks of further bloodshed, willing to commit to a long-term occupation or monitoring of Germany to enforce whatever terms the Germans might accept. Indeed, many Allied politicians, especially in Britain, wanted to see Germany quickly recover, both to restore a balance of power on the Continent and for German consumers to once more be in a position to buy British goods. Britain needed a treaty that kept Germany strong enough to serve as the engine of a postwar European economic recovery but not strong enough to pose a threat to the European political system. It is highly unlikely that any treaty could have negotiated that peculiarly deadly Scylla and Charybdis of the postwar years.

From the perspective of the French, the recovery of Alsace and Lorraine might excite nationalist politicians and serve as a patriotic background for numerous postwar celebrations, but it did not justify the deaths of an estimated 1.4 million Frenchmen. Nor did the French feel safe after 1919. In addition to the strategic considerations outlined, the French knew that they still faced a more populous Germany to their east. They also knew that their former allies were either gone (czarist Russia) or unwilling to sign a mutual security agreement to come to France's help in the future (the United States and the United Kingdom). They also faced the tremendous task of rebuilding their farms, mines, and factories, while those in Germany remained intact. The euphoric mood of November 1918 did not last long.

That the peace conference would take place in Paris was never seriously in doubt, despite the wishes of the British delegation for a smaller and less emotionally charged site. When the British proposed other locations, Clemenceau, as hard-hearted as any politician in Europe, wept. Paris had the advantage of being large enough to host as big a conference as anyone could envision, and it also served as a kind of symbolic reward for the sacrifices of the French people. Paris was, of course, also a traditional capital for diplomacy. Still, British fears that a Paris conference would quickly turn into a circus and a magnet for any group with a grievance were not far off the mark.

People did come to Paris, and they came in droves. The British, who had had fourteen official representatives at the Congress of Vienna in 1815, brought more than four hundred officials to Paris in 1919. The Americans brought with them dozens of advisors, known collectively as the Inquiry. Along with the diplomats came swarms of journalists, politicians, and would-be influence peddlers. They included the young Indochinese patriot Nguyen Ai Quoc, who later changed his name to Ho Chi Minh; the well-connected Romanian queen Marie, who hoped to use her popularity to help her native land come out of the conference strong despite its humiliating defeat on the battlefield; and the Arabian emir Faisal, who came to cash in on British promises that he would control a large Arab state in exchange for his leadership of a revolt against the Ottoman Empire.

But the biggest celebrity of all was the mercurial, contradictory, sanctimonious, and occasionally charismatic American president, Woodrow Wilson. He was the first American president to leave the United States while in office. That remarkable fact had as much to do with American attitudes toward the outside world as it did with early twentieth-century transportation limitations. Wilson received an ecstatic welcome from the people of Europe. At least for a little while, Europeans tired of war and conflict saw him as a potential savior from the old system and a possible architect of a newer, more just world.

But that feeling did not last long. European leaders quickly came to dislike Wilson's constant moralizing, his lack of understanding of the problems of Europe, and his stubborn unwillingness to see the destruction of France with his own eyes for fear, he said, of the devastation hardening his heart toward Germany. By the time the conference ended, almost everyone in Europe, and many members of the American delegation itself, had grown weary of Wilson and frustrated with his ineffectiveness at the conference.

One of those Americans, the future American ambassador to the Soviet Union William Bullitt, resigned before the treaty was finalized and left Paris to, in his own words, "lie on the sand and watch the world go to hell." The Treaty of Versailles is not solely responsible for the hell that Europe and the world did in fact go through just a few years later, but it played a critical role. If we are to understand diplomacy, decolonization, the Second World War, and the twentieth century more generally, there is no better place to begin than with the First World War and the treaty that tried to end it.

True peace did not come to Europe for many more decades, after a second world war and an often precarious Cold War. During the latter, the presence of American and Soviet forces kept Germany and France from even thinking of continuing their feud. The integration of their armed forces into alliances controlled by the superpowers removed the possibility of their acting with military force against one another. On a more positive note, the increased integration of their economies into the European Union gave them incentives to opt for peace rather than conflict. Over time, the people of France and Germany themselves came to reject the very idea of war against one another, choosing instead to open the border between them, share a currency, and coordinate regularly on foreign policy. The Treaty of Versailles can take no credit for any of these positive reforms, except perhaps as a warning from history of what not to do.

It is not the point of this book to rescue the reputation of the Treaty of Versailles. Nor will it make any judgments about who "won" and who "lost." With the perspective of a century, it seems quite obvious that the Treaty of Versailles produced a legion of losers and precious few winners. This book has a more modest goal. It will offer a brief introduction to the complex world of 1919, the individuals who played starring roles in that year, and the many factors that produced this treaty. We can debate the abiding influence of the treaty on the world we inhabit today, but there can be no doubt about its importance in shaping the twentieth century.

Chapter 1

From war to armistice
to peace conference

Contrary to what German nationalists said both during the war
and after, the combined Allied armies had decisively defeated the
German army on the battlefield by the summer of 1918, and the
German senior leadership knew it. The turning point came in July
at the Second Battle of the Marne. After that point, the Germans
won no more battles, and the generals started to watch their
military power evaporate while the Americans landed tens of
thousands of fresh soldiers every week. As early as August,
German army commanders had concluded that the combination
of the collapse of their Austro-Hungarian and Ottoman allies,
American entry into the war, Allied material superiority in
airplanes and tanks, and turmoil inside Germany itself made
it highly unlikely that Germany could emerge from the war
victorious. As the crisis grew and problems mounted, they warned
Kaiser Wilhelm II that his soldiers would no longer fight for him
or for the monarchical system he represented. Mutinies by
soldiers and sailors alike sealed Germany's fate. By October,
the senior military leaders of Germany had begun to urge their
government to make peace under almost any terms the Allies
offered in order to salvage what they could from their wartime
gains in the east and to prepare to confront the possibility of a
Bolshevik-style revolution at home.

Allied leaders were, for the most part, just as surprised as the Germans by the sudden approach of the end of the war. Though they shared the goal of defeating the Germans, they agreed on little else. The Americans, new to the coalition and growing stronger by the day, wanted to keep fighting, driving the war into Germany itself even if that meant continuing combat operations into 1919 or even 1920. They had a plan to do just that, with armies of well-supplied and well-trained soldiers backed up by the latest mechanized vehicles, including enormous air armadas and fleets of tanks. The American commander, Gen. John Pershing, citing "the experience of history," warned of being too eager for an early armistice and of overestimating the remaining strength of the German army. He advocated instead forcing the Germans to accept an unconditional surrender on German soil.

His views had few supporters in 1918, especially among the people who had been fighting for four long and bloody years. The British and French, exhausted from bloodshed and recognizing the risks of carrying the war onto German soil, sought an early end to the fighting that would establish clear conditions for diplomats and statesmen to sign a permanent peace that would end the war on terms favorable to the Allies. They hoped to do so before the winter of 1918–19 gave Germany a much-needed period of recuperation and an opportunity to transfer soldiers from Russia and Ukraine to France and Belgium. British and French generals also recognized that a peace signed in 1919 or 1920 would increasingly come on American terms, and they recognized as well that, unlike the United States, they would have to live alongside the Germans when the war ended. They therefore hoped to get an armistice that would make it impossible for Germany to resume combat operations on land or on sea. Once accomplished, and with Germany's allies seeking armistices as well, the diplomats could get to work on the terms of a final treaty.

The man who had to make the final decision that autumn, Allied supreme commander and French marshal Ferdinand Foch, tried

1. Paris held a massive victory parade on Bastille Day, 1919, that passed, appropriately, through the Arc de Triomphe. By the time of the parade, however, many people in France and Europe more generally had begun to doubt whether the peace so recently achieved would hold.

to draw a sharp distinction between an armistice and a final peace treaty. Hoping to keep the politicians out of his business, he insisted that an armistice was an agreement concluded between soldiers. It should end the military phase of the war and put in place the conditions to guarantee a durable victory on the battlefield. A favorable armistice would prevent Germany from restarting hostilities and would provide the foundation for a permanent postwar peace that would guarantee France's future. Foch saw no benefit, but considerable risk, in American ideas for invading Germany itself. As he told Woodrow Wilson's representative in Europe, Edward House, he was not fighting a war for the purpose of killing. Once he could obtain a sufficiently favorable armistice, Foch said, he had no right to shed any more blood. As a result, he concluded, largely symbolic gestures like an invasion of German soil did not justify any further loss of human life or the risk of the fortunes of war turning against the Allies.

Throughout September and October 1918, as a German defeat began to look ever more likely, Foch worked with his staff to draw up armistice terms. Although he consulted with French government officials, he largely kept them at arm's length, neutralizing even Prime Minister Georges Clemenceau. He also shut Pershing out of the process. On October 8, Foch submitted to the French government a memorandum arguing that the Allies could agree to an armistice only if the Germans agreed to evacuate all the territory they had taken since 1870 (to include Alsace and Lorraine); to permit three Allied bridgeheads over the Rhine River in order to facilitate an invasion of Germany, should it later become necessary; and to surrender all military and transportation equipment in place rather than transport it back to Germany.

Clemenceau and the senior representatives of the British and American governments did not openly disagree with most of Foch's terms. They were, however, nervous about a military man making decisions with such enormous political implications. As British prime minister David Lloyd George said, "I admire and love Marshal Foch, but on political questions he is an infant." Foch, however, was far from an infant. Clemenceau saw him more as an imp, playing a dangerous political game best played by the adults. Clemenceau determined to keep Foch away from the proceedings at the peace conference, using Foch's own logic against him. If the armistice was an agreement between soldiers, then the peace treaty was an agreement between politicians. Like Clemenceau, Lloyd George and Wilson were determined to keep decision-making to themselves. Wilson spoke to his brilliant and insightful military advisor, Gen. Tasker H. Bliss, only five times during the entire conference. Lloyd George consulted his military advisors even less.

The American and British generals largely accepted, albeit bitterly, their reduced role once the armistice came into effect. The politicians occasionally called them in for technical advice but rarely consulted them on any matters not strictly military in nature. Bliss did receive an invitation to be one of the United States' five plenipotentiaries at the peace conference, but the British did not accredit a military advisor among their five. Clemenceau intentionally snubbed Foch by submitting his name sixth on the French list of five. Foch grew frustrated, and even before the conference began, he started to meddle in political

2. Clemenceau speaks to the German delegates at the anticlimactic signing ceremony for the Treaty of Versailles, which took place in the same room where the Germans had finalized their victory over France in 1871. The symbolism was supposed to underscore how the tables had turned, but instead it projected an image of vengeance.

affairs in the Rhineland, encouraging Rhenish separatists and
assigning to the Rhineland occupation bridgeheads senior
French officers who shared that view. The resulting rift between
Clemenceau and Foch never healed.

The tension between the "brass hats" (the generals) and the "frocks"
(the politicians) formed an important subtext in the period
between the armistice and the peace conference. Foch knew that
his armistice terms were harsher than British politicians wanted
and not in the same spirit as the peace notes that Wilson had sent
to the Germans in October through the Swiss chargé d'affaires in
Washington. The president's first note was a reply to overtures to
the Americans from Prince Max of Baden, who tried to convince
Wilson that Germany was willing to end the war based on the
principles of Wilson's Fourteen Points. Max headed a group of
German moderates who had seen the Fourteen Points as a
way to protect Germany from the worst elements of French and

3. **Gen. Tasker Howard Bliss (center) was among the military officers
who tried to warn the diplomats of the errors they were making. Like
most generals, he had a hard time making his voice heard at the peace
conference.**

British vengeance. A generous, pro-German interpretation of some of the points also implied that Germany might keep any parts of their conquests where large German minorities resided, including Poland, the Baltic states, and maybe even Alsace-Lorraine.

On October 8, about the same time that Foch was finishing his armistice memorandum, Wilson replied to Max in a measured tone that seemed to open the door to a compromise peace, maybe even the "peace without victory" of which Wilson had recently spoken. The Germans were elated, seeing a chance to salvage something from their military defeat as well as a way to drive a wedge between the British and French on one side and the Americans on the other. Not surprisingly, the British and French governments reacted angrily, both at the lenience of Wilson's reply and the decision of the president to communicate directly with the Germans without involving, or even informing, them. Both to mollify his allies and in anger at news of continued German sinking of merchant ships, Wilson wrote a much harsher note to Max on October 14, insisting on an end to Germany's "illegal and inhumane" military operations as well as evidence of democratic reforms inside the German government. A third, equally harsh, note soon followed just in case the Germans were confused about which Wilson note better represented the president's thinking.

Wilson's harsher tone in the final two notes surprised the Germans and seemed to end the plan of playing Wilson against the British and French. It also led the Germans to accept an armistice as inevitable, although they continued to hold out hope that it might still be based on Wilson's principles. The Germans soon moved to make political changes that could show Wilson that they were serious about democratizing their system as the president had demanded. The abdication of Kaiser Wilhelm II and his exile into Holland in the first days of November helped them make that case. Whether it would make any difference in the final armistice terms remained an open question.

On November 7, 1918, the Germans formally requested negotiations for an armistice. They still hoped that such negotiations would be a genuine discussion and that the terms of an armistice would be based on the Fourteen Points and the spirit of Wilson's first note. The new German politicians saw such an armistice as the best, possibly the only, way out of their strategic dilemma. The senior German military leaders, on the other hand, saw any capitulation to the Allies as unacceptable, notwithstanding their own acknowledgment of the inevitability of military defeat. Gen. Erich Ludendorff, recognizing the inevitability of defeat, fled in disguise to Sweden on October 26 and soon began to perpetuate what became known as the "stab in the back" myth that Germany had been betrayed at home rather than defeated in the field.

For his part, Foch had no interest in an armistice on Wilson's terms, nor did he believe that an armistice was ultimately within the purview of politicians. He directed a German delegation of five representatives to a forest clearing near Compiègne and was furious to discover that the Germans had sent four unknown politicians; consistent with Foch's understanding of the process, the Allied delegation contained only military officers. Just one German general came to Compiègne, and none of the Allied generals knew who he was, although they were angry to see that he wore a medal given to him by the French before the war for his service as an attaché. Foch ordered him to surrender the medal before he would open any discussions about an armistice. He wondered whether this delegation of unknowns really spoke for Germany and whether they would be able to hold Germany together at the end of the war.

In no mood for compromises and suspecting some sort of German ruse, Foch offered the German delegation no negotiations over the terms of the armistice; they could accept the terms he and his staff had devised or the war would continue. The final terms included German evacuation of Alsace-Lorraine, Belgium, and the Rhineland; surrender of almost all German ships, airplanes, and heavy guns; renunciation of the treaties Germany had imposed on Russia and Romania; and construction of Allied bridgeheads across the Rhine River. The German delegates were stunned by the severity of the terms but saw no choice. They signed the armistice on November 11, 1918, ending the shooting but leaving the terms of the final peace still to be determined. Foch believed that he had done his part of the job by destroying the German military and making it certain that the Germans could do no more physical harm to the Allies. As he told Clemenceau, "My work is over. Yours begins."

Foch was well aware that the armistice could do little to address some of the many destabilizing forces inside Europe that the war had unleashed. Among the most threatening was Bolshevism, the revolutionary ideology that had overthrown the Russian provisional government in 1917 and appeared to be gaining adherents across the Continent, most threateningly in Germany itself. The rise of left-wing movements inspired the formation of right-wing movements to counter them, most importantly the violent paramilitary German units known as the *Freikorps*. The risk of civil war and revolution in Germany, Italy, Hungary, and elsewhere threatened to unbalance any agreement the victors tried to impose. For this reason, Foch permitted the Germans just one modification to the armistice terms: he allowed them to keep some of their machine guns in the event that they might be needed to stop a Bolshevik revolution inside Germany.

The growing threat of Bolshevism hung menacingly over the period between the armistice and the peace conference. Bolshevism, and the particular brand of it that the Soviet Union represented, posed a challenge to more than the capitalist economic and social order in the West. It also threatened the international colonial order. Shortly after taking power, the Bolsheviks had published secret treaties signed between the czarist government and its British and French allies. These treaties deeply embarrassed Western governments, revealing as they did the naked power grabs that had characterized great-power wartime diplomacy. They also undermined the noble principles for which the British and French governments claimed that they were fighting. Most importantly, in October 1917, the Bolsheviks published the text of what became known as the Sykes-Picot Agreement of 1916 in which the British, French, and imperial Russian governments had divided much of the Middle East among themselves. Russia was to get Istanbul and the Turkish Straits, Britain modern-day Jordan and Iraq, and France modern-day Syria and Lebanon.

The revelation of Sykes-Picot did more than make a mockery of British and French principles. It also allowed the Bolsheviks to depict themselves as the true champions of oppressed peoples looking to free themselves from European imperialism. Sykes-Picot seemed to show the bankruptcy of British promises to Arab and Zionist leaders to help them create states or homelands in the same areas the British and French were claiming as their own. People across the globe saw the hypocrisy of British and French actions in the Middle East and took notice. Bolshevik leaders hoped to attract Asian and African allies with promises of support and denunciations of the European imperial model.

Woodrow Wilson worried that the Bolsheviks might present a viable alternative to his own anti-colonial ideals. Wilson spoke often of fixing national borders along ethnic lines (the popularization of the phrase "national self-determination" came a bit later), and his Fourteen Points called for righting the wrongs of the colonial system; however, he was himself too much of a racist to believe that most non-Europeans were ready for self-government. He did not even believe that the Irish were ready to rule themselves, let alone the Koreans, Egyptians, or Senegalese. Nevertheless, Wilson did not want to lose the global battle for the hearts and minds of people in Africa and Asia to the Soviet Union. He still hoped that people around the world would see the United States, not the Soviet Union, as their champion, even though he knew he needed the support of the British and French to make his plans for the postwar world come to fruition. The Bolsheviks, on the other hand, were quite ready to combine anti-colonialism with a class-based understanding of the global order that attacked the British and French for exploiting subject nations around the globe. They were also prepared to think about rapid, even violent, change where Wilson hoped for slow, evolutionary change.

No one in the West quite knew how to read the new political environment in Russia. The Romanov dynasty had disappeared forever as a political force in Russia, but conservative counterrevolutionary "White" forces still had the strength to defeat the Bolshevik "Reds." Some in the West, led by Winston Churchill, wanted to support the Whites in the brewing Russian civil war, even if that meant accepting a Japanese intervention into eastern Russia and supporting right-wing groups in the Baltic states as allies. Churchill boldly called for strangling Bolshevism in its cradle. Advocates of a strong policy in Russia worried that the Bolsheviks posed as great a threat to the West as the Germans had before the war. They often called for offering lenient peace terms to Germany in the hope that Germany might provide a strong counterweight to Soviet Russia. Critics countered that the Whites were reactionaries unlikely to help move Russia forward and, if victorious in the civil war, would likely impose a harsh system based largely on the czarist model.

Arguments for intervention won the day even if no one could quite foresee what sending a relatively small Allied force to Russia might actually accomplish other than helping a beleaguered Czech legion trapped behind the lines. In the fall of 1918, Great Britain, the United States, Canada, and France sent almost fourteen thousand soldiers to the frozen White Sea port of Archangel (Arkhangelsk), ostensibly to secure lines of communications, but in reality to offer support to the Whites. The expedition was never popular or effective. It highlighted the ongoing problems the West had in formulating consistent policy toward Russia. Lacking reliable information on events there and unsure of how to respond, the leaders of the peace conference decided not to extend an invitation to Paris to the same Whites they were theoretically supporting, nor did they accredit any White diplomats as representatives of a Russian government in exile. The White leadership's internecine struggles for power, antidemocratic political attitudes, and inability to defeat the Reds did not do much to make them seem like feasible partners in the postwar world.

Russia remained the giant red elephant in the room throughout the Paris Peace Conference. No peace in Europe could long endure without Russia at least acquiescing in its terms, but without any representatives at the conference, the Russians would not have an incentive to accept a treaty that they had had no part in negotiating. The Allies never considered inviting Vladimir Ilyich Lenin, Leon Trotsky, or any other Bolshevik representative to Paris. They continued to see the Bolsheviks and their call for class warfare as a mortal threat to Europe. Nor did they see the logic in talking to the same Bolsheviks that they hoped would soon fall from power. As a result, neither the Germans nor the Russians were represented in Paris, even though small states such as Peru, Guatemala, and Haiti were. Many people recognized the problem even if they could not formulate a solution to it.

The ideas of Woodrow Wilson served as a different kind of challenge to the Europe Foch and other conservatives hoped to create. Millions of Europeans found Wilson's support for national self-determination and a supranational body to arbitrate disputes appealing. Millions more around the world found his ideas about decolonization attractive. Wilson himself understood that the United States had to provide an alternative both to old Europe and to the new Bolshevik regime if it hoped to assume a leadership role in the postwar world. Wilson's own allies, however, recoiled at many of his ideas, especially those that might weaken

French or British power in the postwar world. For his part, Wilson recognized the conflict between his own idealism and the realpolitik of the French and British, but he expected that his ideas would prove so appealing to the people of Europe that their leaders would have little choice but to follow his guidance.

Domestic politics also played a role in shaping the coming conference, as two of the great democracies went to the polls before the opening of the peace conference. The United States held midterm congressional elections on November 5, 1918. They resulted in a gain of five seats in the Senate and twenty-five seats in the House of Representatives for the Republican Party. Wilson, a Democrat, therefore faced a hostile Congress, especially in the Senate, where the gain of five seats was sufficient to give the Republicans control of the all-important Foreign Relations Committee, which held the constitutional obligation of ratifying any treaty Wilson negotiated. The new chairman of that committee, Massachusetts senator Henry Cabot Lodge, distrusted Wilson's principles and despised him on a personal level. Lodge once told Theodore Roosevelt that he never expected to hate anyone as much as he came to hate Wilson. He pledged to make Wilson's job at the peace conference extremely difficult by blocking any treaty that did not meet with his approval. Lodge and those who thought like him opposed any limits that the treaty or an international body like the League of Nations might impose on America's right to act unilaterally. They especially worried that such a body might commit the United States to foreign conflicts not in the nation's interests. Lodge eventually led a group of senators, known as the Irreconcilables, who pledged to prevent the Treaty of Versailles from even coming up for a vote in the United States Congress.

Wilson might have chosen to respond to his party's electoral defeat by asking some prominent Republicans to accompany him to the peace conference. The mutual hatred between Wilson and Lodge made choosing the latter impossible, but there were other options. Former president William Howard Taft, for example, emerged as a possibility. Taft had shown great interest in foreign affairs, and he shared some of Wilson's goals, including the formation of the League of Nations. He had also worked with Wilson during the war as the chairman of the National War Labor Board. But Wilson was not in the habit of listening to his own advisors, let alone those of another party. Nor was he in much of a mood to offer an olive branch to Lodge or the Republicans who had sworn to oppose his most cherished ideals. The poisonous relationship between the executive and legislative branches of the United States government left deep and lasting legacies.

Elections affected the peace treaty on the other side of the Atlantic as well. In the United Kingdom, a general election in December returned the wartime coalition government, with David Lloyd George continuing as its prime minister. The election produced a general consensus in Britain to force the Germans to pay for the costs of the war. One prominent politician campaigned with the slogan, "We shall squeeze the German lemon until the pips squeak." Conservative newspapers took up the theme as well. Lloyd George himself had promised to make Great Britain "a land fit for heroes." Part of that pledge meant ensuring that Britain came out of the peace conference with tangible gains to redeem its enormous sacrifices and German money to pay its debts. Whether Lloyd George could deliver on those promises to the satisfaction of the British people was an open question as the conference commenced.

Planning and hosting a peace conference of the size and scope necessary to end the Great War took approximately two months. The delay had several important consequences. Most notably, the armies of the victorious nations had begun rapidly to demobilize. Having believed that the war had ended on November 11 with the signing of the armistice, the British, French, and American people not unreasonably demanded the return of their sons, brothers, and husbands. Politicians had little choice but to go along, both to satisfy voters and to reduce the crushing expenditure of maintaining large armies. But the quick melting away of Allied military strength created a problem for the diplomats about to work out the terms of the peace. Without large standing armies, how would the victorious powers respond if Germany refused to sign the final treaty or resumed hostilities? The armistice itself had to be renegotiated periodically, as the one signed in November was due to expire at almost the same time the conference began. What if negotiations to extend the armistice failed or the German state fell victim to a Bolshevik revolution? Would there be sufficient military power left to compel the Germans to behave as the Allies desired? Would the British and French people consent to a call from their governments to remobilize?

In order to maintain power over Germany in the absence of large armies, the Allied naval blockade of Germany remained in place until the Germans signed the final peace treaty. As a result, food and medicine could not flow freely into Germany. Most Allied officials saw the shortsightedness of this policy, especially as influenza took a huge toll on Germany, and by extension to France and other neighboring countries as well. American officials, including future president Herbert Hoover, worked hard to try to find ways to bring food into Germany, but they had only limited success. The continuation of the blockade, even after most people believed that the war had ended, increased the illegitimacy of the peace process in the eyes of most Germans, and many people outside Germany as well, even before the conference itself began. Allied policy looked more like vengeance than peacemaking.

The two-month delay also gave the diplomats time to think about what kind of conference they wanted to host. The most recent conference of its type was the Congress of Vienna, held at the end of the Napoleonic Wars. A British academic wrote a history of that conference at the request of the British and French governments, but even he doubted that any of the delegates in Paris bothered to read it. If they had, they might have learned much of value, including the ways that the differing goals of allies can create friction, the desires of small and large powers to use the conference to air long-standing grievances, and the danger of raising false hopes of the conference producing eternal peace. The men of 1919, however, saw their task as entirely different from that of 1815. To cite one example, the Congress of Vienna had included the defeated French in the hope of rehabilitating the Bourbon dynasty overthrown during the French Revolution. In 1919, by contrast, there was no desire to include the Germans in the peace conference or to restore the defeated Hohenzollern dynasty. To the contrary, people in France and Britain were talking about dragging Wilhelm from his exile in Holland and trying him for war crimes.

The Congress of Vienna dealt with territorial issues far from Europe. Similarly, the Paris Peace Conference also sought to remake the entire globe, although on different principles. Given the nature of the British and French empires and the universalist nature of Wilson's ideas, the globalization of the peace conference was probably inevitable. Every country that had sent men and money to contribute to the defeat of Germany believed that it had a right to be a part of the conference. In the end, thirty nations sent official representatives. They included dominions of the British Empire, including New Zealand, Canada, and Australia, which were no longer willing to be represented in international affairs through the British Foreign Office, as they had been before 1914. They also included states as small as Siam, Cuba, and Liberia, all of which had declared war on Germany. Many of these states came with mutually contradictory demands, notably in the Balkans and Eastern Europe, where wars and armed conflict continued despite the armistice. Japan and China, too, both sent representatives to Paris, forcing Europeans to arbitrate between the two countries' mutually exclusive demands.

This internationalism created enormous problems, especially given the shallow knowledge most diplomats had about events far from Europe. Statesmen therefore had to make decisions about places they had never visited and about which they often knew virtually nothing. Paul Cambon, a veteran French diplomat, watched in befuddlement as he saw "the shambles, the chaos, the incoherence, and the ignorance" about the world that marked discussions even before the conference's opening. Because the great powers had refused to set a formal agenda for the conference (for fear of limiting their options too much), the proceedings threatened to ramble aimlessly around the world's problem spots making mostly uninformed decisions that would affect the lives of millions of people. Much of the hard work of the conference thus fell to committees of lower-level officials, some of whom had real knowledge about the problems they were studying; others just had an axe or two to grind.

The world had already changed a great deal in the time between the armistice and the opening of the peace conference. The growth of Bolshevism provided a dark backdrop to an already dark postwar European picture that included an influenza pandemic, civil wars, and the possibility of wars between some of the potential successor states to the Austro-Hungarian Empire over future borders. The political contexts in the United States and Great Britain threatened to further complicate matters, and tensions between the civilians and their military officers simmered just below the surface. Nevertheless, hopes remained high that the leaders of the United States, Great Britain, France, and Italy could somehow work through these problems and give Europe the peace it so badly needed. It was an awesome responsibility to give to any group of leaders, not least to the four heads of government who assembled in Paris in January 1919 to do, as British diplomat Harold Nicolson wrote, "great, permanent, and noble things."

Chapter 2
The big three
(or maybe four)

In the early months of 1919, David Lloyd George, Woodrow Wilson, and Georges Clemenceau together held as much influence over world affairs as any three men in history. They had the power to redraw borders, determine forms of government for foreign countries, and influence the destinies of people around the world. Historians can make too much of the importance of individuals in shaping history, but there is no denying that these three men played enormous roles in the final outcome of the Treaty of Versailles. There can be no understanding of the peace conference or the treaties it produced without an understanding of these three men, what they had in common, and the areas where they disagreed.

All three represented democracies, although they had taken different routes to power. Lloyd George came out of the coal-mining communities of Wales and had championed the cause of working people against the privileges of the commercial and landed elites. As chancellor of the exchequer in the years before the war, he had helped to usher in many elements of the British welfare state. He had also made many enemies, especially among Britain's conservatives, for his financial policies, his desire to curb the power of the House of Lords, and his outspoken opposition to Britain's prosecution of the Boer War in South Africa. His antiwar speech in Birmingham in 1899 caused a riot that led to the deaths of two people and forced Lloyd George himself to escape from the hall disguised as a policeman. His opposition to the Boer War notwithstanding, he was not a pacifist. He did, however, oppose unjust wars fought for the purpose of extending the empire's reach or for the benefit of financial markets. The outbreak of war in 1914 led him to ask some deep and probing questions about how and why it began, but he never questioned the basic wisdom or necessity of Britain's engagement in it, however ominous and fateful he thought the war might be.

The German invasion of Belgium convinced Lloyd George and many other politicians from his Liberal Party that Britain had no choice but to fight. He argued in a critical speech in August 1914 that his support for Britain's war against Germany reflected the same ideals that had let him to defend the Boers, namely the immorality of the strong dominating the weak by means of military force. As Britain had unjustly gone to war with the Boers, so, too, had the Germans unjustly invaded Belgium and France. He saw more quickly than most that the war would not end in a few short months and that Great Britain would therefore need to prepare itself for a long, costly conflict. He rejected Prime Minister H. H. Asquith's 1914 call for "business as usual" and worked instead to bring centralization and modernization into British industry.

Despite the enemies he had made over his years of political infighting and accusations that he had more mistresses than principles, Lloyd George took on increasingly important roles during the war. His understanding of the demands of modern war and his background in coal country gave him distinct advantages as his responsibilities over the British wartime economy increased. He became the inaugural minister for munitions in 1915, charged with modernizing weapons manufacturing, and then the secretary of state for war in 1916. Even his critics came to respect the way he reorganized British industry, bolstered the morale of the workforce (despite his calls for limiting the hours British pubs could remain open), and projected his faith in final victory. He showed a willingness to work with groups as diverse as suffragettes and the opposition Conservatives to pursue the shared national interest in the defeat of Germany. By 1918 he was, and at least for a few months longer would remain, a popular and deeply admired leader who came to the Paris Peace Conference able to boast of having a mandate from his people to speak on their behalf.

Although the two men were very different people, Lloyd George's path to the peace conference shared much with that of his French counterpart, Georges Clemenceau. Both were from poor places relatively isolated from the centers of power. Lloyd George hailed from Wales and Clemenceau from the Vendée in western France, a region with a reputation for its unstable political atmosphere. Like Lloyd George, Clemenceau had also made enemies among his country's conservatives, in Clemenceau's case for his opposition to the privileges of the wealthy and the Catholic Church. He had been a prime leader of the movement to exonerate the falsely accused Alsatian Jewish officer Alfred Dreyfus, whom the French army had tried to frame for treason in the 1890s. He, too, had a reputation for fierce political infighting and had fought many duels in his younger days. As a journalist, he had used his newspaper to bring down numerous French governments of which he disapproved. His great rival, French president Raymond Poincaré, once said of Clemenceau that he was a man made for catastrophes: if he could not prevent them, he would provoke them.

Clemenceau and Lloyd George may have been deeply unpopular with conservatives in their own countries, but they both had solid reputations as patriots. Clemenceau had been the mayor of the Montmartre section of Paris during the Franco-Prussian War and had opposed the peace treaty with Germany that resulted in the surrender of Alsace-Lorraine. As early as September 1914, he had emerged as a vocal and intense critic of the French government for not fighting the war with sufficient ardor and competence.

In return the government heavily censored his newspaper, *L'Homme Libre (The Free Man)*. Clemenceau responded by renaming the paper *L'Homme Enchaîné (The Man in Chains)* and maintaining his criticisms despite pressure from the government.

Lloyd George had developed a similar reputation for patriotism. He became known for his speech at Mansion House in 1911 defending the rights and honor of Great Britain on the world stage. The speech came in the midst of a diplomatic row between France and Germany. It pledged British support for France, and Lloyd George's service during the war further showed that, despite his criticisms of the British establishment, he was as dedicated to the British cause as anyone. Unlike Clemenceau, however, Lloyd George was a member of the British government in 1914. He therefore worked within the system rather than from the outside.

Somewhat to the surprise of many of their fellow countrymen, Lloyd George and Clemenceau both rose to head their governments before the war's end. Lloyd George became prime minister of a coalition government in December 1916, and Clemenceau returned to that job in France (he had been prime minister from 1906 to 1909) in November 1917. Both men advocated fighting a war to the end against Germany. Clemenceau also became the war minister as well as prime minister. When asked for specifics of his policies, he often said simply, "Je fais la guerre" (I make war). Lloyd George solidified political alliances with British conservatives, won over key newspaper barons, and extended Britain's war in the Middle East as well.

Both men also showed a willingness to stand up to their generals and impose their own view of grand strategy, a foreshadowing of the way they isolated their military advisors at the Paris Peace Conference. Neither man showed much deference to the military expertise of the generals, as their predecessors had done. Instead, they often made strategic decisions contrary to the desires of those

The big three (or maybe four)

33

same generals. Lloyd George took military forces in Belgium and France away from British Expeditionary Forces commander Gen. Sir Douglas Haig, a man he despised and derided. Against the advice of most of Britain's senior military officers, Lloyd George sent forces later in the war to Italy and to Palestine, hoping to find victory somewhere other than the frustrating western front. In Palestine, at least, he got what he wanted, as British forces seized Jerusalem, setting up both British power in the region and conflicts with the French in the months after the war. He also touched off a furor inside the British army in the spring of 1917 when he temporarily put British forces under the command of the French general Robert Nivelle. That idea proved ill-fated, as Nivelle's offensive failed miserably, leaving behind tensions between Lloyd George and the generals that never healed.

Clemenceau had the benefit of having seen the Franco-Prussian War and having covered the end of the American Civil War as a young reporter. These experiences, plus his natural aversion to the conservatives who ran the army, made him more than willing to challenge his own generals. Clemenceau forced his will on military strategy, kept officers from playing key roles at primarily political bodies like the Supreme War Council, and coined the phrase that war was too important a business to be left to generals. He instinctively understood the essential insight of the Prussian military theorist Karl von Clausewitz that war is at its heart a political act. It therefore needed to have politicians, not generals, directing it.

Nevertheless, neither man had made his political name on foreign policy or defense issues. Nor had either one traveled much beyond his own borders on official diplomatic missions. Neither one knew much about the complexities of places like central Europe, the Middle East, or Russia. Clemenceau, however, may have had some important insights into the nature of the United States from his time spent there and from his (ultimately unhappy) marriage to an American woman. He may have understood even better than

Woodrow Wilson the significance of the Republican triumph in the 1918 congressional elections. He appears to have grasped with his politician's sixth sense that the election had fundamentally undermined Wilson's position.

Wilson shared the general ignorance of global affairs with his two European counterparts. He had even remarked to a friend on the eve of his inauguration in 1913 that "it would be an irony of fate if my administration had to deal chiefly with foreign affairs." He had given little thought to the rest of the world before becoming president, although he had an unshakable belief in American moral superiority that guided his views of the world beyond America's shores. Although he did not face the risk of his government collapsing as could happen in a European parliamentary system, Wilson was never a popular president. He had won the 1912 election primarily because of a split in the Republican Party, and he won reelection in 1916 by one of the slimmest margins in American history. Wilson had in fact gone to bed the night of the election certain that he had lost. About 2,500 voters in normally Republican California gave Wilson just enough votes to win and thereby avoid the humiliation of becoming only the second incumbent president not to win reelection.

Wilson certainly had his enemies, most notable among them the popular former president Theodore Roosevelt, but he could inspire followers as well. Progressive reformers and journalists often saw Wilson in near-messianic terms as the herald of a new age in American history and maybe the world's history as well. When the moral example of America proved insufficient, Wilson did not shy away from using force, as he did in sending American troops to Mexico, Haiti, and, later, Russia.

Hoping to keep America out of the war in Europe, but sharing his countrymen's general hope for Allied victory, Wilson had played a double game between 1914 and 1917. He called for the American people to be impartial in regard to the war, but he had at the same time defined neutrality in such a way as to allow (or even encourage) American bankers, farmers, and industrialists to profit from the war. For reasons that were both practical and ideological, most American trade went to the Allies. American policy from 1914 to 1917 thus infuriated the Germans, who came to see the United States as a belligerent in all but name. Wilson's policy also angered the British and French, who believed that the United States shared their general war aims but chose to profit from the war rather than commit itself to the shared goal of defeating German militarism.

The tensions in Wilson's foreign policy reflected his uncertain political position at home. Wilson knew that he would face a serious challenge for reelection in 1916, as the split in the Republican Party had healed. Theodore Roosevelt, the man who had caused the split by forming his own party in 1912, had pledged to support the Republican nominee in 1916, in large part out of his desire to see Wilson beaten. He even considered running for president himself. Some surprising losses by Democrats in the 1914 congressional elections seemed to point to Wilson's vulnerability. Although the war in Europe was only one factor among many for the American electorate, it put Wilson in an awkward spot, as he had to navigate between the isolationist wing of his Democratic Party, represented by his own secretary of state, William Jennings Bryan, and the increasingly shrill condemnation of his continued policy of neutrality coming from the Republicans.

The president's response to the German sinking of the *Lusitania* in May 1915, in which 128 Americans were killed, proved to be a turning point for both sets of his critics. Wilson had refused the demands of isolationists to ban Americans from traveling overseas in recognition of the increased risk they now faced and the possibility of a future sinking leading the United States into war. Wilson saw such a move as inconsistent with American honor, a position that led Bryan to resign as secretary of state. On the other hand, Wilson had publicly stated in a speech he gave in Philadelphia that the United States was "too proud to fight," words that filled his Republican critics with anger and shame and led many of the most prominent among them to end their public support of the administration's foreign policy and work for his defeat in 1916.

Wilson had a hard time finding policies that both upheld the nation's honor and avoided American entry into a war he knew the United States was in no position to fight. He mostly drew praise for his peaceful resolution of the *Lusitania* crisis as well as his handling of the 1916 German torpedoing of a civilian ferry ship, the *Sussex*, which injured several Americans. After the *Sussex*, Wilson extracted a promise from the Germans to stop unrestricted submarine warfare. The Sussex Pledge allowed Wilson to position himself in 1916 as the candidate of peace and to use the campaign slogan "He Kept Us Out of War," even though Wilson knew that he could not continue his diplomatic balancing act forever. With each act of German aggression, his strategy of demanding concessions without threatening war would grow less and less effective both at home and abroad. When the Germans resumed unrestricted submarine warfare in February 1917, thereby invalidating the Sussex Pledge, most Americans saw that war with Germany had become inevitable. Wilson still held out hope that he could avoid war as he had done in 1915 and 1916, but the release of the Zimmermann Telegram, in which the Germans proposed an anti-American alliance with Mexico and Japan, severely limited his options.

Wilson's responses to American entry into the war in April 1917 reveal a great deal about his views toward war and the way he wanted to shape the peace that would follow. Much more than Clemenceau or Lloyd George, Wilson believed that wars came from regimes, not peoples. Freely elected governments, he said, did not send their citizens off to war in the modern age except in self-defense. The problem in Germany was not the German people, therefore, but their aristocratic and unrepresentative government. Change the government by deposing the kaiser and instituting true democracy, and the German people could assume their rightful place in Europe. Thus in his declaration-of-war speech he emphasized, "We have no quarrel with the German people. We have no feeling towards them but one of sympathy and friendship. It was not upon their impulse that their Government acted in entering this war."

Neither Clemenceau nor Lloyd George shared Wilson's version of recent history. While both distrusted the kaiser's government, they saw other causes at work. Like most British strategists, Lloyd George believed that the traditional European strategic balance of power had failed. One state (in this case Germany, abetted by Austria-Hungary and the Ottoman Empire) had grown too powerful to be contained or deterred by the prewar alliance system that the great powers had so carefully crafted. In the postwar era, he believed, a Europe dominated by a too powerful France could be just as unstable as the prewar era had been. Thus the British had opposed the detachment of the Rhineland from Germany as, in Lloyd George's words, an Alsace-Lorraine in reverse. For the same reason, the British were reluctant to commit to a permanent alliance with France in the postwar years.

Clemenceau laid the blame squarely at the feet of the Germans, a state and a people that had, in his view, been an existential threat to France since its unification in 1871. Fueled by a hyper-nationalist ideology and powered by a highly industrialized economy, Germany had chosen to threaten and bully its neighbors. Only an international coalition working together in a four-year total war could stop it. Clemenceau did not share Wilson's hope that a democratic government could properly channel the energies of the German people, nor did he put much faith in the Germans accepting their defeat and reforming themselves. He demanded protections from Germany for his native France, which, unlike the United States or Great Britain, still had to live next door to its traditional enemy.

4. Most Germans saw the Paris Peace Conference as illegitimate and one-sided. The most reactionary among them turned to violent paramilitaries such as the Freikorps, whose poster reads, "Protect Your Homeland."

Although there were no socialists among the plenipotentiaries of the great powers, they offered a different opinion on the causes of the war. They tended to believe that the war had been caused by the concentration of wealth and power that resulted from the inherent nature of the capitalist system. The profiteering of arms manufacturers and imperialists had created conflict between the great powers that eventually spilled out into a global war. The Big Three, as Wilson, Lloyd George, and Clemenceau came to be known, successfully kept such ideas out of the conference rooms, but they knew how popular those same ideas were with segments of all of their populations.

Each leader's views about how and why the war had started naturally influenced ideas about the peace. Wilson came to be the leader of an ideology called liberal idealism, or internationalism, that called for the creation of structures above the nation-state. Advocates believed that such a system could resolve disputes before they turned into wars. They also argued that building institutional networks of cooperation (most importantly through global trade) between nation-states would give states incentives to work together instead of seeing the world as a zero-sum game. Wilson thus championed the formation of a League of Nations, an idea that had its origins in the late eighteenth century but had languished until the war seemed to show the need for some supranational body that could help the world avoid future catastrophes.

Clemenceau and Lloyd George did not necessarily oppose the formation of an international body, but they did not believe that such an organization could or should replace the role of the nation-state. Clemenceau in particular wanted the League of Nations to act as a kind of permanent international alliance against German resurgence. Neither he nor Lloyd George put much faith in the effectiveness of the League of Nations to fulfill Wilson's vision, but, knowing how important it was to the president, they used their support for it as a bargaining chip. So, too, did the Italians and Japanese, both of whom occasionally threatened not to join the League unless they obtained some of their key demands in return.

Nor could powerful states be expected to cede some of their power to an international group unless they could control its outcomes. The League had as one of its principles that all states would be represented equally regardless of size, even though five of the nine places in the governing League Council would be held by the war's great victors. Lloyd George, Clemenceau, and Henry Cabot Lodge all thought an egalitarian structure foolish, as it would inevitably dilute their own states' power. Many Europeans also wanted to keep the Russians and Germans out of the League until they adopted democratic forms of government. But the more states that stayed out of the League, the less power and legitimacy it would have.

The Big Three dominated the Paris Peace Conference, but they were not alone. Italy believed that it deserved a place at the table and significant rewards for its declaration of war against Austria-Hungary in May 1915. Italy's prime minister, Vittorio Orlando, styled himself the "Premier of Victory," but his position at the conference was weak. The British and French especially resented Italy for, in their view, auctioning off Italy's services to both sides before deciding that the Allies could offer them more than the Germans could. Italy's mediocre performance on the battlefield and its need for massive Allied aid after the collapse of the Italian army at the Battle of Caporetto in October 1917 further undermined the Italian position.

Orlando also had severe political and personal limitations. He spoke little English and only halting French but did not like having to rely on translators, so he rarely used them. He was himself a member of the Italian Liberal Party but had to work with the powerful Sidney Sonnino, the foreign minister and a former prime minister. Sonnino was a member of the opposition Historical Right Party, which had major foreign policy disagreements with the Liberals, especially in their demand that Italy annex Dalmatia and Fiume. The Big Three were staunchly opposed to those annexations; thus Orlando found himself in the awkward position of having to balance the obstinacy of his allies with the demands of his own government. He also knew that if Italy did not come out of the conference with tangible gains, the constitutional monarchy itself might not survive an armed challenge from the left or the right. At one point during the conference, the stress led him to break down sobbing in front of his fellow statesmen, underscoring their view of him as an amiable gentleman but a hopelessly weak politician. He walked out of the conference in protest in April and then resigned as prime minister on June 23, just before the signing of the Treaty of Versailles. He did not attend the signing ceremony.

Sonnino proved to be even more difficult for the Allies to deal with than Orlando. On the surface, Sonnino might have been the kind of man to get along with the Big Three. He was in fact half Welsh, which might have endeared him to Lloyd George. He was also, like Lloyd George and Clemenceau, an outsider, half Jewish by birth and Protestant by faith in an overwhelmingly Catholic country. But Sonnino shared none of Wilson's ideals, did not defend Italy's positions well, and always seemed to be asking for much more than the Big Three thought Italy deserved. They were soon wistful for the days when Orlando represented Italy in Paris.

Any Italian statesman would have found himself in a difficult position in Paris. Uncertain of popular support for Italian entry into the war, the government had promised a quick march to Vienna followed by massive gains for Italy in the Trentino, the Adriatic coast, and even parts of the Ottoman Empire. But the war had turned out to be bloody and inconclusive, with a stalemate in the Julian Alps alongside the Isonzo River. The collapse at Caporetto led to the change of government that brought Orlando to power, and it also led to a new military command structure. The Italians ended the war with a major victory over exhausted Austro-Hungarian forces at the Battle of Vittorio Veneto, raising Italian hopes for the peace conference.

Such hopes, unrealistic though they were, inspired such Italian demagogues as the poet and aviator Gabriele d'Annunzio and the journalist and war veteran Benito Mussolini. They called for massive expansions of Italian territory and threatened violence against the government if it did not find some way to achieve them. They pledged to oppose with force the proposed creation of a large Slavic state opposite the Adriatic Sea from Italy. Some had begun to talk of a "mutilated victory" and *spazio vitale* (vital living space). They came to see Britain and France as enemies of Italy for denying Italy its just compensation for its wartime contributions. Although the French and British did not see just how unstable Italian hyper-nationalism would become, Orlando and Sonnino did. They also knew that strong Italian opposition to the creation of Yugoslavia would force them to take a harsh line against it despite the Big

Three's support for it. Orlando refused to meet with the Yugoslav delegates and even went so far as to call them enemies of Italy.

Some non-Europeans played key roles as well. Jan Smuts, a former Boer commander, parlayed an unusual political career into a prominent role at the conference. Fearing a German takeover of South Africa in 1914, then seeing a chance for South Africa to conquer German colonial possessions in Africa, Smuts rose by 1917 to a seat on the Imperial War Cabinet, where he became a critical advisor to Lloyd George, despite turning down Lloyd George's offer to become commander of British forces in the Middle East. Smuts wanted South Africa to take over German Southwest Africa (later Namibia), but he also favored lenient terms against Germany more generally and supported the League of Nations. He eventually became the key advocate of the mandate system by which the British and French took over effective political control of large parts of the former Ottoman Empire.

5. South African Jan Smuts was one of the few important non-European voices at the conference. He was largely responsible for the mandate system that decided the fate of the former German and Ottoman colonies.

As a group, the men in positions of power in Paris believed deeply in the superiority of white people, whether in Virginia, Palestine, or Namibia. They occasionally listened politely to the entreaties of people from Africa and Asia but rarely took their opinions or their concerns seriously. They never did grasp how deeply the four murderous years of the war had undermined the ideals of European superiority on which their empires had been constructed. They still believed themselves to be at the top of the evolutionary pyramid and therefore to still deserve the right to shape the destinies of people around the globe, even without seeking their consent. With the possible exception of Woodrow Wilson, they also believed that having suffered deep human and material losses, their societies were entitled to a share of whatever spoils were to be had.

The one exception to this general pattern of European feelings of superiority over the rest of the world involved Japan, which had emerged as a serious rival and occasional partner to the Big Three. Since opening to the West in the 1850s, Japan had modernized and developed into a major power. It had defeated China in the Sino-Japanese War of 1894–95, Russia in the Russo-Japanese War of 1904–1905, and then German forces in China and in the Marshall, Marianas, and Caroline Islands. Thanks to its naval alliance with Great Britain, Japan was also the only non-European state in a formal alliance with a European one. European statesmen were never quite sure whether to read Japan as a looming threat or a potential ally for their own goals of power projection, but by 1919 more of them were coming to the former rather than the latter view.

For their part, Japanese leaders knew that the European influence in Asia would likely decline after the war, and they very much wanted to be the power that would fill in the resulting vacuum. Their delegation to Paris was led by Prince Saionji Kinmochi, a seventy-year-old elder statesman and former prime minister who had studied at the Sorbonne and had been a classmate of Georges

Clemenceau there. Japanese leaders mistrusted the principles of Woodrow Wilson, seeing right through his noble-sounding ideals to the racist core that underlay them. As one Japanese newspaper wrote, Wilson was an angel in rhetoric but a devil in deed. The Japanese knew that Wilson held Asians to a lower standard of development than he did Europeans. They also blamed Wilson's promises of national self-determination for the rise in anti-Japanese sentiment in both China and Korea. Hoping to catch Wilson in a trap and expose his hypocrisy, the Japanese delegates came to Paris seeking to force the insertion of a racial equality clause into the final treaty. Either the Allies would agree, and thereby undercut their own rationale for imperialism, or they would refuse and give the Japanese a tremendous public relations victory across Asia, especially inside the European and American colonial empires.

The Japanese also came to Paris hoping to increase their influence in the Pacific Rim more generally. The Allies had pledged to give Japan permanent influence or control over any German colonial territories north of the equator that they could capture. Having done its part, Japan expected to be rewarded, not only with those islands, but also with concessions in the indisputably Chinese region of the Shandong Peninsula, controlled by Germany before the war. Shandong loomed as a potential roadblock to everything Wilson wanted to accomplish. Unquestionably Chinese, it might have to be placed under Japanese control in order to assure Japanese participation in Wilson's cherished League of Nations.

But if the Big Four (if one wants to be generous and include Italy's Orlando) were powerful, they were not omnipotent. They all came from fractious, democratic political systems with many overlapping and contrasting interest groups. Their citizens by no means agreed on what they wanted to see the peace conference accomplish. Many of them had already become deeply disillusioned with the very systems the Big Four represented, and

6. The leaders (left to right) of the United Kingdom, Italy, France, and the United States—David Lloyd George, Vittorio Emanuele Orlando, Georges Clemenceau, and Woodrow Wilson—largely set the agenda for the conference. They were not, however, omnipotent, as changing circumstances and competing interest groups limited their decision-making power.

a violent minority of them, from both the left and the right, had begun to plot revolution. The Big Four thus had enormous challenges ahead of them as they sat down in Paris not only to try to resolve the problems of the world but to satisfy the hopes of their own people as well.

Chapter 3
Ideals versus interests

The stories of how three powerful, egotistical men collided, disagreed, and grew tired of one another during the stresses of a six-month diplomatic conference make for fascinating reading. Georges Clemenceau, for example, battled both David Lloyd George and Woodrow Wilson, as well as his own generals, to push through his vision for the security of France. He survived an assassination attempt by a deranged Frenchman along the way, and his sharp wit and acid tongue made him seem larger than life. When his finance minister, Louis-Lucien Klotz, made a simple mistake during one session on reparations, Clemenceau complained to Lloyd George in full voice that he was unlucky enough to have as his financial advisor the only Jew in Europe who knew nothing about money. Coming from a man with a well-earned reputation for protecting the rights of Jews in France, the comment was all the more surprising yet, at the same time, typical of Clemenceau.

Clemenceau and Lloyd George understood each other well enough. Both were old veterans tempered in the world of European politics and knew how to play the game. They had also worked together in the war's final months to achieve a common victory against both the Germans and, sometimes, their own generals. They certainly had respect for one another, although whether they genuinely liked each other is much harder to determine and probably irrelevant in any case. They may in fact have been too similar to develop a true fondness for each other.

They represented states that, while in the same victorious coalition, did not share fundamental goals for the postwar world. The British people especially mistrusted French aims and worried that the treaty might weaken Germany so much that France would grow too powerful both in Europe and overseas as a result. From the British perspective there seemed little reason to defeat a German bid for hegemony only to see a French one emerge in its wake. The American general Tasker H. Bliss noted only half-jokingly that as a result of the divergence of British and French interests, making peace with Germany would be easier than making it with America's allies.

Bliss's president, Woodrow Wilson, was in many ways the outlier of the group. Having never seriously considered the problems of Europe before 1914, he came to the conference the least informed of the senior statesmen. Recognizing his own limits, he had formed a group called the Inquiry to advise him. He filled this group with academics and regional experts who he hoped could give him sufficient background information to make decisions of global import. Still, the members of the Inquiry got precious little of the president's time, nor did Wilson seem terribly interested in working through the specifics of the myriad problems of Europe. Instead he told the members of the Inquiry, "Tell me what is right and I will fight for it." Whether such a principled stand would suffice to solve the many problems that the war had either created or exacerbated remained one of the great questions in Paris in 1919.

Standing on principles prevented Wilson from using his most powerful tool, Allied war debts. The British and French together owed more than $7 billion to the United States government and $3.5 billion more to American banks. American promises to restructure or forgive parts of that debt could have provided

Wilson with sufficient leverage to obtain almost any concession from the Europeans that he might have wanted, but Wilson chose instead to appeal to what he hoped was a European desire to remake the world along Wilsonian lines. His firm belief in laissez-faire capitalism also undercut any use of debt to enforce political change because to do so meant risking the stability of global markets. If Wilson could not get a new Europe from Lloyd George and Clemenceau personally, he expected that the popularity of his ideas among the European people more generally would achieve the results he wanted. The rapturous receptions that Wilson initially got from the war-weary European people on his arrival could only have reinforced that belief. Consequently, like the good son of a Presbyterian minister that he was, Wilson sought to persuade rather than compel his counterparts to see the world the way he himself saw it.

Few Europeans expected Lloyd George or Clemenceau to stand on idealistic principles. Wilson, however, had made so many idealistic (and sufficiently vague) statements about self-determination and the righting of past wrongs that millions of people across the globe thought that he was speaking to their particular grievance. He seems to have recognized the false hopes he had inspired, especially since he did not believe that his ideas applied to most non-European peoples. He told his propaganda chief, George Creel, "I am wondering whether you have not unconsciously spun a net for me from which there is no escape." The remark is typical Wilson, blaming others for problems of his own making while simultaneously trying to soften the blow with the use of the word "unconsciously."

His comments to Creel notwithstanding, Wilson came to Paris believing himself a savior to the world. The self-image did not always inspire others. One British diplomat said that Wilson appeared in Paris with the air of a debutante "entranced by the prospect of her first ball." He was simultaneously arrogant and ill-informed, a combination that baffled his European interlocutors.

Lord Robert Cecil, the British under-secretary of state for foreign affairs, spoke for many when he described Wilson as a bully unwilling to compromise or even listen to the ideas of those better informed on a given topic than he was. Cecil had been an early champion of the League of Nations but grew disenchanted by Wilson's unwillingness to listen to the League's constructive critics, even those who shared most of Wilson's own goals for the organization. Cecil also grew frustrated with Wilson's ignorance of the important technical and legal details necessary to bring the League to fruition. On this and many other matters, Wilson only concerned himself with the loftiest of ideals, leaving to others the hard work of putting his ideas into operation.

Another French or British politician might well have done in broad outline what Clemenceau or Lloyd George did, but no other American politician would have approached his role in Paris in the way that Wilson did. Had Theodore Roosevelt or Wilson's 1916 presidential rival, Charles Evans Hughes, been president it is easy to imagine an American position based more on power and a willingness to compromise rather than the uninformed idealism and personal stubbornness of Wilson. Those few voters in California in 1916 who turned the election to Wilson likely changed history much more than they could possibly have realized.

The personalities and interactions of the Big Three are fascinating, but there are other ways of seeing the workings of the Paris Peace Conference. One of the most intellectually profitable is to examine the difficulties involved in finding ways to replace four of the great Continental empires that had governed Europe for centuries, namely the Romanov (Russia), Hohenzollern (Germany), Habsburg (Austria-Hungary), and Osman (Ottoman). Few people in 1914 had expected these empires to disappear, not even the people who most ardently wished for their destruction. Even the youngest of the dynasties, the Romanov, had existed since 1613. The oldest, the Osman, dated to 1299. Even those who had referred before the war to the Ottoman Empire as the "sick man of Europe" or the Habsburgs as being on the wrong side of history had difficulty envisioning that one of them, let alone four of them, would disappear in a matter of just a few short years.

One person who had predicted their demise, Friedrich Engels, had written that a future European war would be "condensed into three or four years and spread all over the continent: famine, epidemics, general barbarization of armies and masses, provoked by sheer desperation; utter chaos in our trade, industry and commerce, ending in general bankruptcy; collapse of the old states and their traditional wisdom in such a way that the crowns will roll in the gutter by the dozens and there will be nobody to pick them up." Prophetic though those lines are in retrospect, Engels had written them in 1887, and yet the empires had survived for more than two and a half decades longer. They seemed in 1914 to be permanent fixtures on the European and global stages despite their inherent weaknesses and occasional struggles to deal with the pressures of modernization and nationalism.

By the time of the Paris Peace Conference, however, the Romanov, Hohenzollern, Habsburg, and Osman empires were all either already confined to the dustbin of history or (in the case of the Osman) well on their way to that ignominious fate. As Engels had predicted, there was no one willing to pick up the crowns and no one willing to follow them even if someone did. Finding a way to replace the empires would be a monumental task on an order of magnitude unprecedented in European history.

Except for the unquestioned assumption in Paris that Alsace and Lorraine would return to France, redrawing the map of Europe presented far more questions than answers. At least four different rationales for the shifting of post-imperial borders in Europe presented themselves. Unfortunately, they often stood at cross purposes to one another. The most obvious, and most traditional, one would award the winners pieces of territory taken away from the losers. Thus Italy demanded the Trentino, large slices of

Dalmatia, and even parts of Anatolia. France put in claims for control of the coal-rich Saar region on the basis of compensation for the damage that the Germans had done to French coal mines. Britain and France also moved quickly to claim former German colonies in Africa, and much of the scramble for power in the Middle East centered on the desires of the British and French to annex the pieces of the now-defunct Ottoman Empire. In those cases, the delegates to the Paris Peace Conference did not care about the self-determination wishes of the people living in those regions. In East Asia, Japan demanded concessions in the Shandong Peninsula and control of Germany's Pacific island colonies as compensation. Conversely, Bulgaria and Hungary, both on the losing side, expected to face territorial losses.

This system of victors taking spoils was at least as old as European diplomacy itself. In the last round of major European wars (1864–71), Prussia had taken territory from Denmark, Austria, and, of course, France. Under the rules of the old game, French seizure of the Saar would have been logical and normal. But Woodrow Wilson claimed that he had come to Paris to prevent just such a repetition of the old European way, which he saw as a background cause of the region's wars. The United States therefore did not make any territorial claims despite its own use of such claims in recent wars with Mexico (1846–48) and Spain (1898). Wilson hoped to establish a new precedent in international affairs and enforce a second rationale for peacemaking, national self-determination. In theory, national self-determination would align ethnic groups with nation-state boundaries both to reduce causes of conflict and to provide political representation to groups that felt that the old empires had denied it to them.

In theory, the idea of national self-determination held great appeal. In practice, it proved maddeningly difficult to administer. To cite just one complex example, Wilson had pledged in Point Thirteen of the Fourteen Points that "an independent Polish state should be

7. British minister Herbert Samuel (in white pith helmet, center) went to Palestine to help Britain replace the Ottoman Empire's influence there. The Paris Peace Conference made decisions that ranged across the globe, often with unforeseen results.

erected which should include the territories inhabited by indisputably Polish populations." But finding borders that would satisfy Wilson's requirement without at the same time alienating German, Ukrainian, and Russian minority populations would prove to be quite a challenge to an Eastern Europe that had developed under imperial, not nationalistic, lines. There was thus no "indisputably Polish" (or, for that matter, indisputably Ukrainian or Czech or Serbian) part of Europe to which all could agree. Populations were too intermingled in most parts of Europe to provide for the clean, easily demarcated borders that national self-determination required. Furthermore, many people had never identified themselves with a nation-state, only with a region or a religion or a language group. How could diplomats in Paris categorize people who did not themselves know to which nation they wished to belong?

The question of what exactly constituted a nation could plague even a seemingly open-and-shut case like Alsace-Lorraine. The French claimed that the region was not open for discussion on grounds of national self-determination because Prussia had illegally seized it in 1871. But many Alsatians did not see themselves as either French or German. Did the Alsatians therefore constitute a separate nation? What about the Germans who had lived in Alsace since 1871 and comprised a majority in many Alsatian towns? Should their rights count, or were they recent arrivals transplanted by an acquisitive German regime to cement its own influence in the region? And if one accepted the logic that the Alsatians were a separate nation, then what about the Irish, who could also claim that their land had been illegally and wrongfully taken? Did centuries of Protestant Anglo-Irish residence in Ireland give Protestants rights akin to those of the Germans in Alsace? Wilson himself denied that the Irish formed a separate nation, claiming that they were really British. Who then were the Corsicans, Bavarians, or Albanians?

Even if one could somehow define what constituted a nation based on criteria like religion or language, how could the Big Three define borders for those nations? Every part of Europe had historical debates about who rightfully owned the land and what groups rose to the ill-defined level of "nation." The leaders at the Paris Peace Conference could not possibly have cut all those Gordian knots, and even if they could, they could never have satisfied everyone. Still, Wilson had raised expectations across Europe and across the world, as his comment to Creel attests. In Point Ten he had written: "The peoples of Austria-Hungary, whose place among the nations we wish to see safeguarded and assured, should be accorded the freest opportunity to autonomous development." But who exactly were those peoples, which ones should get their own state, and where should their borders be? Were the Czechs and Slovaks similar enough to warrant their inclusion in the same state? What of the German, Polish, and other minorities who would inevitably be included in those borders? Where to find the "clearly recognizable lines of nationality" that Wilson demanded for the borders of Italy in Point Nine? What to do about the maddeningly complex problems of a polyglot place like the Balkans?

Most claims for territory came with either a historical or an ethnic argument. In the majority of cases, of course, the historical positions of one group contradicted those of one of its rivals. The Poles and Italians especially made grandiose claims for land based on ancient ownership, angering the Western diplomats charged with drawing the borders. Even Italy's Vittorio Orlando realized the difficulty of making such claims when he joked that by the standards of some of the historical demands being made, his country ought to recover all of the lands once ruled by the Roman Empire. It was easy enough to reject some claims, like the one by French reactionaries that the Rhineland was French because it produced more wine than beer, but few cases were so absurdly clear-cut. Indeed, what part of Europe could not be claimed by multiple groups if one went back far enough into the historical record?

A diverse and heterogeneous Europe thus presented a multitude of challenges, especially to statesmen not familiar with its contours. More than once, a region in dispute would come up for discussion only to have several senior delegates confess that they had never heard of it. At other times, they wondered if they were not creating future disputes like the one over Alsace and Lorraine that had destabilized Europe in the aftermath of 1871. Nationalists in many parts of Europe pledged that they would not accept any borders that left fellow countrymen living outside them, even if they were minority populations in the places in which they lived.

Personalities mattered as well. The Czechs had articulate representatives who agreed on the main points of the Czech position and showed a willingness to compromise with their future neighbors. The Poles, on the other hand, disagreed even among themselves about the borders of both historical Poland and the new Poland they wished to create. Two mutually antagonistic Polish delegations pushed their cases so far that they angered not only the diplomats in Paris but their new neighbors as well. Jan Smuts gave up on them all, calling Poland a historic failure. Other groups, such as the Kurds, were absent from Paris and therefore unable to plead their case.

One possible solution to the dilemma of the diversity of Europe lay in conducting plebiscites, essentially asking the people of a region what kind of future they wanted for themselves. Even this solution, however, proved difficult. Because most self-identified Frenchmen had left Alsace-Lorraine after 1871, a plebiscite there would likely return a vote for Alsace-Lorraine staying inside Germany, an outcome totally unacceptable to the French. Because the expected results of plebiscites often ran counter to historical claims of other states, they could be sources of conflict as much as sources for solutions. Nor did the British and French necessarily like the precedent that plebiscites set, for fear that people in Ireland, Corsica, India, Indochina, or maybe even Lloyd George's native Wales might demand a plebiscite of their own. Thus, however much Wilson might have pushed for national self-determination as the best way to reorganize Europe, it alone would not solve the problem.

A third rationale rested on strategic grounds. In short, the new states needed to have borders that they could defend. They also had to be able to play a role in stabilizing and balancing the postwar order. France especially looked to sign alliances or agreements with the new states of Eastern Europe in order to help balance Germany and possibly the Soviet Union as well. Big states could fill that role better than small states, even if making them larger worked against the Wilsonian goal of national self-determination. Thus Romania more than doubled in size despite having done little to contribute to Allied victory and despite the fact that most of the territory it added contained non-Romanians. Thus, too, the Allies decided to create one large Yugoslavia rather than several

Balkan states, notwithstanding the historical animosity among groups like the Bosnians, Serbs, Croats, and Montenegrins.

Because the new states had to defend themselves, mountains, rivers, canals, and railroad lines took on enormous importance regardless of the ethnic identity of the people living nearest to them. Thus the new Czechoslovakia obtained control of the mountainous Sudetenland, even though it had large numbers of ethnic Germans. In 1919, this decision was not as controversial as it later became because the new state could not otherwise have defended itself and the Czechs promised cultural autonomy to the German minority. Still, it highlighted the contradiction between ethnic and strategic rationales for redrawing borders. It also underscored the problems of using national self-determination as a guide to national frontiers.

So, too, did discussions over the Rhineland. The people there were ethnically German and clearly identified themselves as such despite their vineyards. Still, as long as it was part of Germany, the Rhineland could present a threat to French security. A cabal of French conservatives, with Foch's acquiescence, tried to encourage a Rhenish separatist movement, promising to exempt a future Rhenish state from postwar reparations in exchange for the Rhineland agreeing to tie itself to France via a collective security agreement and a customs union. Clemenceau found out about the schemes and put a quick stop to them, but the incident revealed the tension between strategic and ethnic rationales and led to one of the important outcomes of the treaty, the demilitarization of a Rhineland that stayed inside Germany.

A fourth rationale was economic. In short, there was no point in creating states that could not feed themselves. To return to the Polish issue, Wilson's Point Thirteen called for Poland to "be assured a free and secure access to the sea." But few Poles then lived near the coast, which was populated mostly by ethnic Germans. The obvious port for the new state, Danzig (Gdansk), had a German majority. To refuse it to Poland would deny the new state a chance to sell its goods overseas, but to take it away from Germany would violate the principle of national self-determination. The same problems confronted Memel (Klaipėda), which had at least a plurality of ethnic Germans, but Lithuanian nationalists demanded it on historical and economic grounds.

These battles over economic issues were anything but trivial. States that could not support themselves would not be able to contribute to the overall recovery of European markets, assist in the restoration of international security, or fend off destabilizing challenges from the left or the right. It is therefore not surprising that so many of the most acrimonious debates about territorial borders occurred over regions rich in coal or other minerals. In most cases, these claims contradicted the principle of national self-determination. To return to the ever-complex Polish case, the Poles demanded Upper Silesia just as the French had demanded the Saar. Both regions contained rich coal deposits, but neither had majority Polish or French populations.

One of the more intractable problems centered on the coal-rich Silesian duchy of Teschen, today the region around Cieszyn near the intersection of the borders of Poland, the Czech Republic, and Slovakia. Another of the places Lloyd George said he had never heard of, Poland demanded it based on a 1910 Austro-Hungarian census that claimed Polish as the dominant language of the region. The Czechs, however, disputed that claim, arguing that most of the region's Poles were newcomers who had arrived to work in the mines; they claimed that the region's true identity was indisputably Czech. The main rail lines of the region, moreover, went to Czech and Slovak districts, not Polish ones.

Under Austro-Hungarian rule, these distinctions did not much matter. In October 1918, however, two rival councils, one Polish and one Czech, had claimed the right to govern Teschen in the wake of the collapse of the empire's authority. Armed forces from both sides had clashed in January and February 1919, auguring a future of violence and instability that might undermine whatever the statesmen agreed to in Paris. These types of incidents also led to a serious disillusionment among senior officials over the idea of creating the new nations and the very concept of self-determination. The American general Tasker H. Bliss wrote to his wife in late February, just as the dispute over Teschen was heating up, that "the 'submerged nations' are coming to the surface and as soon as they appear, they fly at somebody's throat. They are, like mosquitos, vicious from the moment of their birth."

That no group of statesmen, even one highly principled and well informed, could have solved such problems only speaks to the limits of trying to understand the Treaty of Versailles exclusively through the lens of the personalities of the diplomats. They themselves knew that they did not have the requisite knowledge to resolve disputes such as the one over Teschen. For reasons of their own, the British and Americans favored the Poles, and the French favored the Czechs. They all knew, moreover, that once the conference ended, Teschen would be quite far from Paris and London, to say nothing of Washington. Thus whatever they decided was unlikely to last unless the people and leaders of the region themselves bought into it. Under pressure from the Big Three, Poland and Czechoslovakia agreed to an inter-Allied commission that eventually divided Teschen and its coal fields into two with little regard for the ethnic distribution of the town's population. Poland got the city center, Czechoslovakia got the railway. In 1938, as part of the Munich Conference's infamous division of Czechoslovakia, Poland annexed the rest of Teschen, then called Zaolzie. A final resolution did not come until 1958, almost four decades after the Treaty of Versailles and, of course, after another world war.

No one in Paris seriously considered the forced removal of people in order to make the political and ethnic borders of Europe match more closely. Although they became a feature of the post–Second

World War peace process, mandatory removals struck the diplomats of 1919 as inappropriate. Removals would also have required huge numbers of troops to enforce, with the possibility of extended violence resulting. In 1922 and 1923, however, Greece and Turkey did effect just such a removal, as 1,500,000 ethnic Greeks left Turkey and 500,000 Muslims left Greece.

Neither plebiscite nor ethnic removal nor inter-Allied commission could have satisfactorily resolved the two most controversial disputes on the conference agenda, Fiume and Shandong. The economic development of Fiume (today Slovenia's Rijeka) had been one of Austria-Hungary's main industrial projects; it eventually became one of southern Europe's largest ports and a commercial rival to places like Marseille and Naples. With the town's economic boom came migration and population growth from all across the empire, including thousands of ethnic Italians, Croats, Hungarians, Slovenes, and Germans. As in Teschen, rival administrations moved in to govern Fiume as Austro-Hungarian authority disintegrated. Italy claimed the right to Fiume based on the majority Italian population in the city itself, but the new Kingdom of the Serbs, Croats, and Slovenes (soon to be called Yugoslavia) countered that most of the Italians were recent arrivals and that, in any case, the surrounding region was overwhelmingly Croatian and Slovenian. Italian threats to boycott the League of Nations and Orlando's departure from Paris in April in protest of Allied opposition to Italian claims to Fiume made it that much harder for the Big Three to make decisions that had a chance of surviving.

Halfway around the world, a similar situation developed over the Shandong Peninsula. Almost entirely Chinese by ethnicity, it had been under German control until Japanese troops seized it early in the war. By all Wilsonian logic, the transfer of Shandong to full Chinese sovereignty should have been a foregone conclusion. But Japanese troops held the region and were determined to establish exclusionary economic concessions there. Like the Italians in regard to Fiume, the Japanese delegates threatened to withdraw their support for the League of Nations if they did not get effective control of Shandong. The obvious unwillingness of the Big Three to give Japan its other diplomatic aim, a racial equality clause, made it all the more difficult to deny it Shandong as well.

Many important mid-level officials in Paris hated what they saw happening. They knew that the Big Three were leaning toward giving in to Japanese demands because Britain and Japan had a naval alliance and Wilson was cowed by the Japanese threat to boycott the League of Nations. Japan in 1919 certainly looked to be the strongest Asian power; the Big Three therefore had an incentive to minimize conflict with Japan for as long as possible. Still, allowing Shandong to become the sacrificial lamb to Japanese imperialism meant invalidating every principle Wilson and the Americans had come to Paris to enforce. Both Tasker H. Bliss and Secretary of State Robert Lansing considered resigning in protest if Japan got what it wanted in Shandong, though neither actually did. Bliss wrote a sharp letter to Wilson that urged him to call Italy's and Japan's bluffs and, if necessary, form the League of Nations without them. Bliss was also furious with the secret, back-room way in which the Big Three debated Shandong. "It can't be right to do wrong even to make peace," he wrote. He predicted that decisions made on any basis but self-determination would only sow seeds of future problems.

Bliss also worried that the Big Three were fueling future crises by choosing sides and sending surplus weapons to the armies of the new states. "The arms which we brought to Europe in order to kill militarism and to bring an era of lasting peace," he complained to Robert Lansing, "we are going to sell over the bargain counter to the new nations which we boasted that we were going to usher into a world of peace." Better, Bliss argued, to dump the weapons into the Atlantic Ocean as American ships returned to the United States.

Fiume and Shandong removed whatever idealism had remained when the conference opened. With hopes so high in January, it

Ideals versus interests

was inevitable that some level of disillusion would set in. As Bliss himself realized, part of the problem came from the attempt of the Big Three to adjudicate essentially unresolvable conflicts. American ideals by themselves most certainly could not do so. As Sidney Sonnino shouted at Wilson during one session, "Is it possible to change the world from a room, through the actions of some diplomats? Go to the Balkans and try an experiment with the Fourteen Points."

Teschen, Fiume, Shandong, and myriad other points on the map showed the complexity of the Wilsonian experiment. The fates of Teschen and Fiume eventually fell under the authority of other treaties signed at the Paris Peace Conference, but the statesmen negotiating in Paris in 1919 did not subdivide the issues in that way. They were all subject to the same tensions and contradictions of the ethnic, strategic, and economic rationales. They therefore reveal the countervailing pressures that the statesmen faced as they looked to find solutions both to old disputes and to the new ones that had arisen in the wake of the collapse of the old order. It was perhaps inevitable that unpopular compromises characterized so many of the resolutions they finally decided to try to implement in the Treaty of Versailles.

Chapter 4
Drafting the treaty

By the first week of May 1919, the lawyers, diplomats, and staffers
had a full draft of the Treaty of Versailles ready. Although the Big
Three recognized that it was far from perfect, the Paris Peace
Conference had been in session since January and could not go on
indefinitely. Winter had turned to spring in Paris, but the change
of the seasons had not produced much optimism or hopeful sense
of renewal as the conference had dragged on with much work
still to do. As symbols of how much remained to accomplish,
the Italians were showing signs of anger over Allied refusal to
recognize their claims to Fiume, and in China a series of protests,
some of them violent, had broken out over the news that Japan
would take effective control of the Shandong Peninsula. In March
the German minister of defense, Gustav Noske, had ordered forty
thousand members of the *Freikorps* paramilitary units to use
machine guns, flamethrowers, mortars, and even airplanes against
left-leaning Germans. More than 1,200 of them lay dead. Sooner
or later the negotiations had to end, and the treaty with Germany
had to be signed if any semblance of stability were to return.

On May 7, the fourth anniversary of the sinking of the *Lusitania*,
the Allies summoned the Germans to France for the official
presentation of the terms of the treaty. Clemenceau, Lloyd George,
and Wilson ignored Foch's final urgent plea for detaching the
Rhineland from Germany. The Big Three delivered to the German

government a copy of the terms, which they hoped they could keep secret for a few days. More than 180 German delegates and technical specialists came to France to study the treaty and, they hoped, negotiate with the Allies on some of its most controversial points.

The timing was delicate. Writing at about this time, the Prussian theologian Ernst Troeltsch described a "Dreamland" state in which the German people transferred all blame for Germany's defeat to Kaiser Wilhelm. For a few months after the end of hostilities in November 1918, the Germans believed that the defeat of the old regime had purged Germany of its sins, leaving the German people free to chart a new political course without the weight of the guilt borne by a now disgraced regime. Troeltsch believed that this Dreamland state made it all the more difficult for the German people to accept the full magnitude of their defeat on the battlefield. Instead, they expected that the victorious allies would lay the blame on the kaiser and his retinue, as they themselves did. Wilson's own rhetoric, which sharply divided the German people from their government, gave the Germans reason to think so. But rumors about the contents of the Treaty of Versailles and the unwillingness of the Allies to press Holland to release Wilhelm so that he could stand trial for war crimes came as a great shock and further fed into both the disillusion and the anger among the German people.

The terms of the treaty, moreover, soon leaked out. As the most important story since the start of the war itself, it could hardly have been otherwise. The Paris newspaper *Bonsoir* defied the orders of the French government and published the first part (articles 1–30) of the treaty in late May. Another Paris newspaper claimed that it, too, had articles of the treaty to publish. Even the *Berliner Tageblatt* had pieces of the treaty that it claimed it would soon make available to its readers. Many of the terms of the treaty had already become public knowledge, at least in the form of semi-accurate rumors. The German people were not pleased with what they learned. A crowd gathered in Berlin marching under signs reading *Nur die Vierzehn Punkte* (Only the Fourteen Points), an indication that the Germans might not sign the treaty and a confirmation that the terms were no longer secret. The protests also reminded all concerned that the sands were running out of the hourglass and it was time to bring the treaty negotiations to a definite end.

But if time was short, the treaty was not. As Europeans were learning, the Treaty of Versailles was a massive document that ran to 436 pages containing 433 articles organized into fifteen parts, each focused on a theme. Many of its details were highly technical, dealing as they did with customs unions, financial arrangements, and trade deals. Other articles required a good map and maybe a professional cartographer to interpret as the borders of Europe, especially Eastern Europe, shifted. Few diplomats in Paris in mid-May had seen the entire document and fewer still had read it all. Regional and technical experts had written most of it, with international lawyers sharpening the language where needed. A few of the more grandiose ideas, including Lloyd George's scheme to build a tunnel underneath the English Channel to help Britain rush troops quickly to France in the event of a future crisis, did not make it off the drawing board. Neither did the Japanese request for a racial equality clause.

Perhaps not surprisingly, the treaty's first part dealt with Wilson's prized League of Nations. Because the League would have the responsibility for fixing whatever problems an imperfect treaty left behind, its composition and its structure mattered a great deal. The treaty used the word "Covenant" to refer to the agreement on the formation of the League, thus lending it a religious connotation. As the pious Wilson surely knew, Matthew 26:28 calls for a New Covenant consecrated by the crucifixion of Christ in order to atone for the sins of mankind. After a four-year war of unremitting savagery and cruelty, Wilson saw the League as doing nothing less than atoning for the modern sins of mankind just as

Jesus had died for man's biblical ones. Covenants, inspired as they are by the Divine, are also unchangeable, an interpretation that was to cause the inflexible Wilson a great deal of harm.

The Covenant, in reality a document between lawyers rather than between God and man, gave the League of Nations a broad remit to discuss "any matter within the sphere of action of the League or affecting the peace of the world." It borrowed freely from Wilson's own Fourteen Points, as when it took from Point Four the call for "the reduction of national armaments to the lowest point consistent with national safety." The Covenant hoped to reduce the threat of weapons in part by curbing the "evil effects" that armaments manufacturing could bring to the international system. In this area, as in many others, however, it offered few specifics. The League would be based in Geneva both to give it a neutral air and to keep its headquarters out of the capital cities of the major

8. Paris's Hotel de Crillon, seen here with captured German artillery pieces on display, was Wilson's headquarters for the peace conference and therefore became the center of much activity during the conference. British officials had hoped to meet in a quieter, more isolated city, but the French insisted on Paris.

combatants. The League had thirty-two initial members, including members of the Allied wartime coalition such as Japan and Italy, as well as states such as Siam, Liberia, Uruguay, and China. Canada, Australia, India, and New Zealand all joined in their own right rather than as members of the British Empire. The treaty named thirteen more states for initial membership, including Chile, Persia, and Spain. Neither Russia nor Germany nor Austria were invited to join.

Ironically, given the later rejection of the League by the United States Senate, neither Lloyd George nor Clemenceau had the faith in the League that Wilson had. Clemenceau wanted to see the League become a permanent alliance against the renewal of German power. Most of the Continent's military men doubted whether what Foch called "Geneva chit-chat" could really replace military force as the mechanism for keeping peace in the world. Reducing the armaments of all of the European powers, moreover, meant that despite their wartime triumph, Great Britain and France would not enjoy a superiority over Germany in the postwar world.

The Covenant called for the League to use a series of diplomatic tools, including binding arbitration, as means of resolving future international disputes. Arbitration required all members to plead their cases before impartial judges and abide by their resolution. The idea may seem idealistic or even naive today, but it had proven effective in defusing diplomatic crises in the years before 1914, and several Nobel Peace Prize winners had won their awards for their ideas on the subject. It was, moreover, not too far-fetched a notion to believe that if Austria-Hungary and Serbia had agreed to arbitration in that fateful summer, a major war might never have begun. As a result, a version of the word "arbitration" appears no fewer than seven times in Article 13 alone, and Article 16 proposed that any state going to war without first seeking redress through the League would "ipso facto be deemed to have committed an act of war against all other Members of the League."

The Covenant was not, however, entirely idealistic. Aware of the possible resistance he would face in the US Congress over the League's potential infringement on American sovereignty, Wilson insisted that the Covenant exempt the Monroe Doctrine for, as Article 21 pledged, "securing the maintenance of peace" in Latin America. Thus the United States would still be permitted to exercise its self-appointed right to interfere in the affairs of the region without committing a violation in the eyes of the League or having to submit to arbitration with a Latin American government. Giving the Monroe Doctrine a special exemption not only assured the United States its position of power in its hemisphere, it also underscored the principle that Latin Americans were not able to govern themselves and therefore needed a more "civilized" sponsor. Article 22 applied that same questionable rationale to the rest of the non-European world. It accepted that parts of the former Ottoman Empire, "where their existence as independent states can be provisionally recognized," could govern themselves only subject to the advice of a European country. It was even less optimistic about Africa, noting that most African regions were far from being ready to govern themselves.

Thus emerged Jan Smuts's idea of the mandate system, applicable only outside of Europe. This idea would solve an essential dilemma of the Paris Peace Conference, namely how to administer the former German and Ottoman colonies. As articulated early on in the conference by the British diplomat Sir James Headlam-Morley, "The major point to be determined is whether we propose to take the Colonies avowedly as the natural fruits of victory after a successful war, or to base our claim on the principles of the League of Nations and the welfare of the natives." The mandate system ostensibly answered the question in favor of the latter. Thus the Treaty of Versailles would send a signal that it was creating a new kind of global order, even if real power would not immediately change hands. As even this diplomat recognized, accepting the mandate system "would, in reality, imply little, if any, change in our established methods of administration."

Under the mandate scheme, European states would take on mandatory responsibility to develop a region in the name of the League of Nations. In theory, this system would help to stabilize a region while it learned from a modern, European state how to govern itself. Once it had reached an acceptable stage of development, the mandatory power would yield authority to indigenous governments. Smuts hoped that such a compromise would remove the impression that the British and French had only fought the war for control of more colonies. He and most other British officials spoke more often of the burdens of mandatory responsibilities than the economic or political benefits that might accrue. Thus the Covenant called for the mandatory power to stamp out remnants of the slave trade, stop the flow of opium into international markets, ban child labor, and work to eradicate disease. The mandatory power was also supposed to ensure that legitimate economic markets remained open to all. The League would stand by to monitor progress and to ensure that the mandatory power did not abuse its relationship to enrich itself, but the Covenant established few checks on the mandatory powers, which were almost always Great Britain and France after the United States refused to accept mandates for Armenia or Palestine.

The remainder of Part One and some of Part Two of the treaty settled Germany's borders with its neighbors. Those with France and Belgium generally returned to what they had been in 1870 (France had originally demanded the borders of 1814), thus definitively returning Alsace and Lorraine to France. This part of the treaty also borrowed from Wilson's language in Point Eight of his Fourteen Points. But whereas Wilson had referred to the "the wrong done to France by Prussia in 1871," the Treaty of Versailles cited "the moral obligation to redress the wrong done by Germany" in that year.

The change in wording was subtle, but significant. The Fourteen Points had kept the blame for France's loss of Alsace-Lorraine in the more distant past by citing "Prussia," now no longer an independent state but a part of the unified Germany. Moreover, making use of the passive voice, it did not specify how the wrong of 1871 was to be righted. In some German interpretations, Point Eight even left open the door to a potential plebiscite in the area as a way to right the wrong. The Treaty of Versailles, by contrast, extended the blame for France's loss of Alsace-Lorraine to all of Germany and noted that the residents of the region "were separated from their country in spite of the solemn protest of their representatives." The German seizure of the two provinces thus became a direct violation of the principle of national self-determination. There was, therefore, no mention of a plebiscite or a League of Nations commission for the region. It became French in every respect.

Germany's borders with Poland were far more complex and required more words than those of all the other German borders combined because the new frontiers had to be specified in great detail. The new state of Poland took a large swath of Pomerania, West Prussia, and Posen. The effect was to cut a "Polish corridor" through Germany that would guarantee Poland access to the sea. Poland did not, however, gain control of the overwhelmingly German port city of Danzig, which instead became a free city under the authority of the League of Nations and open for both Germany and Poland to use for trade. Germans who chose to remain living there had to give up their German nationality. East Prussia was thus cut off from the rest of Germany. Memel also became a free city under the protection of the Allies despite the town having a majority German population.

Although buried in the middle of the treaty, the sections on war guilt were bound to draw some of the fiercest criticism, and not only from Germans. Intended to establish a legal basis for the imposition of reparations, Article 231 called on Germany to accept "the responsibility of Germany and her allies for causing all the loss and damage to which the Allied and Associated Governments and their nationals have been subjected as a consequence of the war imposed upon them by the aggression of Germany and her allies." Separate articles called for the creation of tribunals to try war criminals, including Emperor Wilhelm II, "for a supreme offense against international morality and the sanctity of treaties."

Germans reacted angrily to the notion of war guilt, not only out of a sense of honor, but because of their memories of 1914. Most Germans recalled their entry into the war that summer as a response to the decision by Russia to mobilize its armies in support of Serbia. Consequently, Germans from across the political spectrum believed that they had entered the war only as a result of their defensive (and thereby wholly justified) response to the initial Russian provocation. In German eyes, therefore, the blame for the war should fall on Russia and to a lesser extent on Russia's British and French allies, themselves allegedly anxious to use the war to capture some of Germany's wealth and power. Nor did the Treaty of Versailles lay any blame on the Habsburg Empire, which did in fact provocatively and incompetently push the diplomatic crisis of July 1914 to war. This version of recent history had just enough truth in it to make it convincing to the vast majority of Germans in 1919. In any case, the emperors and the regimes that had started the war in 1914 were long gone. To blame their successor states for the damages the war had caused seemed to most Germans an unjustified act of vengeance rather than the proper basis for a postwar treaty.

Those on the left, and not only in Germany, blamed the international system for the outbreak of the war. To single out one state or one regime therefore seemed not to solve the basic problem of Europe. Wilson himself had once pushed this point forcefully, calling for a peace without victors and insisting on naming the United States an associated power rather than a member of the alliance. Blaming Germany alone might satisfy those who wanted revenge or sought financial compensation, but it struck millions of Europeans as inconsistent with the facts of the war.

In keeping with both the internationalist spirit of the League of Nations and the vengeful moods of the Allied leadership, the treaty established fifty-eight international commissions to work out some of the finer points. They were all, of course, dominated by the victorious powers. Commissions determined subjects like setting the exact border between Germany and Belgium; regulating the twin riverine ports of Strasbourg (in France) and Kehl (in Germany); and writing regulations for commerce on rivers like the Elbe, the Oder, and the Niemen that traversed several states or formed parts of international borders. In some cases the commissions made rulings highly unfavorable to Germany, such as the awarding of Malmédy and Eupen, two heavily German regions, to Belgium.

The most important commission of all involved the setting of Germany's reparations payments. Its members would come from the United States, Great Britain, France, Italy, Japan, Belgium, and the future Yugoslavia, with the salaries of the commissioners, their staffs, and all of their expenses paid by Germany. The commission would gather evidence on the resources of the German economy, the amount of damage Germany had done to states it had fought during the war, and the economic needs of the German state. It would also determine which expenses the victors could claim as reparations. Some in France and Britain wanted to include items like the war pensions and medical expenses of soldiers throughout their lifetimes. Others wanted to limit claims to damage to property. The treaty only outlined the first sets of payments Germany would owe, leaving the rest to the commission. It also established that Germany would pay for the Allied occupation of the Rhine River bridgeheads, just as France had had to pay for the German occupation after the Franco-Prussian War of 1870–71.

A commission had advantages that a set figure written into the treaty did not. In theory, if Germany showed itself willing to abide by the terms of the treaty and to become a constructive member of the European community, then the commission could reward it by reducing future reparations payments. On the other hand, the commission could increase reparations and treat them as penalties if the Germans tried to evade their treaty obligations. Critics countered that such calculations were pointless if Germany lacked the capacity to pay the reparations in the first place. Worse still, taking high reparations from a country that could not afford them might lead to famine or political instability; either one might require the League or the Allies to intervene. Reparations might thus provide a kind of catharsis, but they might also make for poor policy, as several delegates to the conference recognized. A commission, rather than a final set figure, provided a way to calibrate future reparations payments to the circumstances of the ensuing years.

Nevertheless, the initial payments called for in the treaty were crippling. By May 1921 Germany was responsible for paying 20 billion gold marks (about £1 billion or $5 billion), with another 40 billion gold marks due in 1926. By some estimates this combined figure of 60 billion marks was just under Germany's annual national income. The treaty gave the commission wide latitude to determine not just the final amounts of the reparations but the interest rates and the methods of payment as well, offering a way to soften the ultimate impact of the reparations. The commission had the authority to transfer German equipment, ships, and other goods as partial payment of reparations. It also oversaw the transfer of tens of thousands of German horses, cows, and sheep to France and Belgium. The treaty called for Germany to give France and Belgium 120,000 sheep, 4,000 bulls, 140,000 dairy cows, and more than 40,000 horses. Germany also had to sell 7 million tons of coal per year for ten years to France at market prices, and 8 million tons of coal to Belgium under the same conditions. These payments in kind could be credited toward German reparations if the commission approved.

These provisions were designed both to impoverish Germany and to compensate France and Belgium for their losses. Other provisions were purely symbolic or just bizarre. Germany had to return all French flags captured during the 1870–71 war, give to the king of Hejaz a historic Koran that the Ottoman sultan had once given to Kaiser Wilhelm, and deliver to the British the skull of the East African king Mkwawa. The Germans had fought Mkwawa as part of their efforts to control the region and force Africans to grow cash crops, especially cotton, for export. Mkwawa led a revolt against the Germans, but in 1898, as German forces closed in on him, he committed suicide rather than surrender. The Germans had taken his skull back to Berlin (or possibly to Bremen) under mysterious circumstances. The British wanted to give the skull to Mkwawa's people, the Wahehe, both as a reward for their cooperation against the Germans during the war and as a visible symbol of the end of German rule in East Africa. The Germans claimed that they could not find the skull, and in the end they refused to comply. In 1956 the Germans sent a skull that may or may not belong to Mkwawa to the new nation of Tanganyika (now Tanzania), where today it resides in a museum in Kalenga.

Other provisions in the Treaty of Versailles protected what we would today call special interests. Brazil received special trade terms for importing coffee into Germany, and textile manufacturers in Alsace received preference in German markets. The treaty also increased international enforcement of the ban on the opium trade, regulated the environmental protection of agriculturally important birds, fixed customs revenues (usually to Germany's disadvantage), and called for the common use of the metric system to replace various local systems still in use. It also dealt in great detail with the provisions of life and fire insurance policies and ensured that the German economy would be open both as a market and as a point of transit for Continental commerce. It therefore insisted on full freedom of overland navigation through Germany, international use of German airfields, and open use of German rivers. Germany agreed to return artworks, archives, legal documents, and economic assets taken during the war. German libraries had to replace books destroyed when the German army burned the

74

Belgian university at Louvain. In some cases, the treaty mentioned specific works of art looted from Belgium or France. It also abrogated nineteenth-century treaties that favored Germany in its dealings with its neighbors; Germany had to renounce no fewer than nine with Luxembourg alone.

The core of the treaty dealt with ways to reduce the power of the new Germany. It annulled all of Germany's eastern gains via the Treaties of Brest-Litovsk (with Russia) and Bucharest (with Romania) as well as attendant financial arrangements designed to give Germany an economic advantage in places like Ukraine. The treaty forbade any territory that had been Russian on August 1, 1914, from ever becoming German and forbade the Germans from building any fortifications that would impede travel into or out of the Baltic Sea. In all, prewar Germany lost about 13 percent of its European territory, most notably to Poland and in the loss of Alsace-Lorraine. Article 80 forbade Germany from seeking to unite with Austria, thus keeping the two great German states and wartime allies apart.

Germany also renounced all claims to its colonies in Africa and Asia as well as any claims to places like Morocco and Egypt where Germany had gained special trading privileges before the war. All German property in those places reverted to the local government. Given the assumptions Europeans made about Africa and imperialism in general, the treaty called on Germany to pay reparations to French citizens in Cameroon for damages done by the Germans during the war, but made no mention of the damage Germany (or, for that matter, the other European powers) had done to the Africans themselves. Nor did the Africans in former German territories receive control over their own destinies. Instead, they became mandates of Great Britain and France. Few Africans would have celebrated the difference.

The treaty made similar paternalistic assumptions about China. Most German properties in China outside Shandong returned to

Chinese control, but the treaty required China to open them to international use, especially in the cities of Hankow and Tientsin. The intention was to create what the Americans called an "open door" for free trade in China. Curiously, the treaty also demanded that Germany return most of the objects its troops had "carried away from China," notably astronomical instruments, during the suppression of the Boxer Rebellion in 1900–1901. Neither the other European powers nor the United States were required to follow suit, even though they had all helped themselves to enormous quantities of Chinese treasures. Economic control of Shandong went to Japan, with enormous ramifications for stability in East Asia.

Reducing the size of the territory Germany controlled represented one stage of the Versailles plan; reducing the power of the German military represented the second key stage. After long debates about how to allow Germany a military strong enough to play a role in European security but not strong enough to threaten the peace, the treaty settled on a German army of no more than four thousand officers and ninety-six thousand men. They could be organized into no more than seven infantry and three cavalry divisions, and they could be trained only "for the maintenance of order within the territory [of Germany] and to the control of [German] frontiers." All German soldiers would be long-serving volunteers rather than short-term conscripts, because of fears that a conscript system would permit Germany to develop a large corps of trained reservists, something the Allies were anxious to prevent. All German ships then interned in foreign ports were to be surrendered and the Germany navy limited to six battleships, six light cruisers, twelve destroyers, and twelve torpedo boats.

Foch saw these limits as political posturing rather than a serious attempt to deal with the military power of Germany. He warned that the British and French governments could not enforce these limits, nor could they enforce the bans on the reestablishment of the German general staff or the construction of submarines, poison gas, military aircraft, and tanks. How, he openly demanded, could the Allies monitor the strength of German telegraphy stations or the types of messages those stations sent, as called for in Article 197? Moreover, what would the Allies do if they found the Germans in violation? Were the peoples of Europe prepared to go to war again over technicalities of a treaty few people would ever read? Even if they were, would the armies of Europe be capable of resuming military operations? He presciently predicted that the Allies would soon find the Germans evading the spirit and probably the precise terms of the treaty, with the Allies incapable of doing anything to stop them.

Many of the articles of the treaty had little directly to do with Germany. The point was to reestablish a new world order (itself a phrase from this era) based on a shared understanding of global ideals. This ideology ran at occasional cross purposes to the vengeance imposed on Germany, making the treaty an odd combination of idealism and revenge, itself a reflection of the varied and conflicting goals that the delegates had for the treaty.

Nationality, which changed as borders changed, was also a prominent problem for the treaty. The treaty offered no guarantees for minority groups like Germans in Alsace-Lorraine or Jews in Poland to have their languages or their cultures recognized by law. Those German nationals living in, for example, the new Poland had to accept Polish citizenship—and thereby renounce their German one—or move to the state in which they had had nationality before 1914. If that solution did not fully line up ethnic and state borders it did, at least, ensure that citizens were not divided by the new borders for the purpose of the enforcement of laws. It did mean, however, that many ethnic minorities were left with few legal protections.

Although primarily a diplomatic document, the Treaty of Versailles covered a wide range of subjects. On issues of gender it looked both forward and backward. It decreed that in all cases of moving borders, a wife's nationality automatically followed that of her husband. From a legal standpoint, therefore, wives had no more say in their nationality than did infant children. On the other hand, it specified that women and men twenty years old and older would have equal voting rights in all plebiscites and elections to determine future borders. These provisions gave women in regions conducting plebiscites greater voting rights than women then enjoyed in France, Italy, or even the United Kingdom, where the 1918 Qualification of Women Act set the voting age for women at thirty. The treaty further specified that all positions at the League of Nations, up to and including the four-person Secretariat that headed the organization, would be open to both men and women. It even called for an investigation into equal pay for women and the mandatory inclusion of maternity benefits for female workers.

Those last two issues appeared as part of the treaty's investigation into international labor. Noting that "the well-being, physical, moral, and intellectual, of industrial high-wage earners is of supreme international importance," Article 427 laid out an agenda for the improvement of the condition of Europe's workers. Intended as a way to undermine the appeal of Bolshevism and especially to win over the loyalties of artisans, these provisions had little directly to do with Germany but had everything to do with the labor unrest in Germany and elsewhere. The article called for laborers to be more than "a commodity or article of commerce" and to be granted full right of association. The article also supported the establishment of "a wage adequate to maintain a reasonable standard of life as this is understood in their time and country," although it offered neither specifics nor a means of enforcement. It did, however, create an International Labor Office to monitor the conditions of workers across the Continent and make suggestions about how to improve them. It also gave the office the power to hear grievances of workers against their own government.

If it did not go as far as some on the left would have wanted, Article 427 did call for an eight-hour workday or a forty-eight-hour work week, at least one full day off (preferably Sunday), and the abolition of child labor. It called for establishing "a system of inspection in which women should take part" in order to ensure that employers respected the rights of their workers. Finally, by calling for equal wages for all workers lawfully resident in a country, the treaty recognized that shifting borders and migratory populations could create a class of exploitable workers in need of protection. Other articles of the treaty guaranteed workers the right to join labor organizations of their own nationality, even when working outside their own borders.

Many of the treaty's clauses created compromises on difficult issues. Critics, including some of the delegates themselves, disliked the abandoning of principles or promises made during the war, but compromise was often the best way out of a sticky situation. Among the best-known of these compromises, Germany retained sovereignty over the Rhineland, thus disappointing those Frenchmen like Foch who wanted to see it become its own country. Articles 42 and 43, however, forbade the Germans from placing troops, conducting military maneuvers, or building fortifications there. In theory, this compromise should have addressed the security concerns of the French (though Foch was far from convinced) while avoiding the creation, as Lloyd George had feared, of a German grievance similar to France's loss of Alsace-Lorraine in 1871.

A similar compromise dealt with the coal-rich Saar Basin, a region that was undoubtedly German by ethnicity but demanded by some French conservatives. It, too, remained part of Germany, but France acquired the exclusive rights to the coal therein "as compensation for the destruction of the coal mines in the north of France" during the war. A commission would govern the region in the name of the League of Nations. After fifteen years, the residents of the region would vote in a non-binding plebiscite to express their desires to the League of Nations about their future nationality. Until then, the region was barred from having fortifications or troops for any purpose other than maintenance of local order. It was a typical Treaty of Versailles resolution, internationalizing a local problem, cutting a compromise that in the end pleased no one, and creating a situation that ultimately proved impossible to enforce.

The treaty thus written, it remained only to be seen if the Germans would sign it. Lloyd George had his doubts that they would. So, too, did the British economist John Maynard Keynes, who worried about what he called "the evil around me." Fear about the consequences of the Germans walking away without signing it left Keynes depressed. It would mean the resumption of the war, the abandonment of months of hard work on the treaty, and the futile waste of the lives of millions.

Chapter 5
To bed, sick of life

Lloyd George and Keynes were right to worry. The Allies were not prepared to resume the war if no German agreed to serve in the role of plenipotentiary or if a German delegation refused to sign once it saw the full treaty. Nor were they ready to handle the possibility of a collapse of the German government. On May 10, Foch had addressed the senior officials in Paris and presented a plan to send forty infantry and five cavalry divisions toward Berlin if the Germans declined to accept the terms of the treaty in full. His plan involved driving through and occupying the Ruhr, then advancing toward Weimar, and eventually capturing Berlin, separating Bavaria from the rest of Germany as he went. Foch predicted a four- to five-week operation—more, he promised, like a military maneuver than a serious combat operation—but he must have had doubts he chose not to share with the politicians. He left Paris for a five-day inspection tour of the Rhine River region to be sure Allied forces had the strength to carry out the plan.

One of the senior British diplomats, Sir James Headlam-Morley, worried that the process of producing the treaty had been too rushed. As a result, he wrote, it "still contains a large number of blunders and some really serious ones" that the Germans would be right to question or at least demand clarification of before agreeing to sign. One such "blunder" involved language in the treaty that could have given the Saar to France permanently, not because it was the intent of the framers, but because of legal ambiguity in the wording. But, he feared, the French would react harshly to any questions the Germans raised and suspect them of trying to prolong the process or evade responsibility. He himself thought that the new borders of Europe were reasonably justified based on the ethnography and economics of the regions concerned but that the peoples of Europe were so mixed that Germany could lodge reasonable complaints. He thought the reparations and the precarious compromises on places like the Rhineland and the Saar were "in their cumulative effect really impossible" for the Germans to accept, but he hoped they would sign the treaty even if there was too little time to correct many of its mistakes. The League of Nations could then get almost immediately to work fixing the myriad problems that a flawed treaty would leave behind.

American officials were hardly any more reassured. Tasker H. Bliss had written to his wife that "No one can tell what is going to happen from day to day. We may have revolutions—I hope not; we may have war again—I hope not." Still, as he watched labor unrest explode into violence in France and as he grew disillusioned with the leadership of Allied statesmen, he worried that revolutions might break out not only in Germany but in France and Italy as well. "If a revolution comes," he warned, "it will not be a gentle one." Looking over the terms of the treaty, Bliss doubted that the Germans would sign and equally doubted that the Allies had the strength to compel them to do so.

The Germans themselves were divided about the wisdom of signing. They had not been present in Paris, but they had a fair sense of the kind of treaty the conference was likely to produce, and they knew that it would not follow the ideals laid out in the Fourteen Points. The head of the German government based at Weimar, Philipp Scheidemann, advocated rejecting the treaty and in fact did resign rather than see his name associated with it. Matthias Erzberger, who had led the delegation to Compiègne for the armistice discussions the previous November, argued for

9. French marshal Ferdinand Foch was the architect of the Allied military victory in 1918. The diplomats saw his role in 1919, however, as meddling in essentially political matters beyond his understanding.

signing the treaty no matter how unfair it might be, then dealing with the effects as best as Germany could. He worried that an Allied invasion of Germany and domestic chaos would follow if the Germans did not sign. For his efforts, a German nationalist assassinated him in 1921.

Eventually, the German government turned to Foreign Minister Ulrich von Brockdorff-Rantzau, who sought a middle position. Like many Germans, he thought of the war as a fair fight that the Germans had lost by bad luck as much as anything. He rejected the Allied claim that Germany and Austria-Hungary were more responsible for the war than Russia, France, or Great Britain, but he was willing to admit German responsibility for its brutal treatment of Belgium. He agreed to go to Paris but had already decided that he had more options other than to sign or not sign. He would instead make the Allies a counterproposal once he had seen the treaty in full, rejecting those demands not in accordance with the Fourteen Points, on the strength of which he believed Germany had agreed to the armistice in November. Like many other moderate Germans, he frequently held out the specter of a Bolshevik uprising inside Germany if the Allies insisted on imposing harsh peace terms. He also warned American officials that Germany would adopt a policy of passive resistance if the terms of the treaty proved to be too harsh.

Brockdorff-Rantzau and his colleagues arrived at Versailles to find their accommodations not quite in accordance with those normally afforded visiting dignitaries. Instead, their rooms were small, in disorder, and surrounded by both guards and a stockade fence. The French had in fact put them in the same hotel the French themselves had used when they negotiated with Otto von Bismarck in 1871. The omens and symbols did not set a positive mood for the discussions. Brockdorff-Rantzau soon found, much to his dismay, that the Allies seemed to have little interest in meeting with him. He feared that he would instead have to give his reply in writing and hope that the Allied delegates would both read it and respond to his demands for a discussion of terms. He eventually wrote Fifteen Points of his own, running to fifty pages in all. He did himself no favors by leaking them to the American press on May 29, before Lloyd George, Clemenceau, or Wilson had a chance to see them.

Nor did he do himself any more favors with the tone of his oral response to the Big Three, who did in the end agree to hear him. Clemenceau, Lloyd George, and Wilson all thought him arrogant. He was long-winded, pedantic, and, to Clemenceau's fury, did not stand when he addressed them. In his three-hour response to the proposed Treaty of Versailles, Brockdorff-Rantzau deplored the one-sided nature of the negotiations in Paris and called for a reassessment of the treaty terms based on the Fourteen Points. He defended the rights of Germans who would soon find themselves outside the borders of Germany, and asked for plebiscites for places like Malmédy, the German-Danish borderlands, and even Alsace and Lorraine. He also opposed the creation of the free states of Danzig and Memel and the placement of Upper Silesia under Polish control on grounds of national self-determination. Finally, he objected to what he knew would be crippling economic conditions imposed on Germany. He ended with a plea to the Allies to live up to their own principles and rewrite the treaty based on common needs in order to shape a durable peace. To the extent that they cared about it at all, French and British officials saw his statement less as a pledge of brotherhood than a threat of violence and noncompliance if the Allies did not give in to his demands.

Brockdorff-Rantzau had done a poor job making Germany's case, and his interpreters had great difficulty translating his legalistic German into the diplomatic French that Brockdorff-Rantzau spoke well enough but chose not to use as a symbol of defiance. Lloyd George said that the speech at long last made him understand why the French hated the Germans as much as they did. Even Wilson, who had tried not to let his emotions get the best of him, said,

"The Germans are really a stupid people. They always do the wrong thing." When Lloyd George asked Clemenceau how he would respond to Brockdorff-Rantzau's speech, Clemenceau merely replied, "I am going to put the treaty under his nose and tell him to sign it."

Back at their hotel, German diplomats and lawyers pored over the text of the treaty word by word. The more they looked, the angrier they grew at its details. Brockdorff-Rantzau became so emotional that the French secret service agents listening in on his room could not make out his words. The Germans saw that any hopes they had of negotiating a Wilsonian peace based on the Fourteen Points had been an unrealizable dream. Back in Berlin, officials of the German government declared the treaty unacceptable and Wilson himself a hypocrite. Predictably, they chose to focus their criticism on Article 231, which established the legal guilt of Germany and its allies for starting the war in order to establish a basis for reparations claims.

While Brockdorff-Rantzau paced and fretted in his hotel in Versailles, the printers were busy producing copies of the complete text of the treaty and newspapers were freely reporting on the details of the terms. As copies of the treaty began to make the rounds across Paris and then across Europe, most informed people were stunned by the sum total of their impact on Germany. The South African statesman Louis Botha compared it unfavorably to the peace treaty that had ended the Boer War. That treaty had established a basis for a future reconciliation between the former enemies Great Britain and South Africa; the Treaty of Versailles did no such thing. Sir James Headlam-Morley wrote home to a friend in England, "While in most cases particular clauses can be defended, the total effect is, I am quite sure, quite indefensible and in fact is, I think, quite unworkable."

The man who was soon to become the treaty's most prominent critic had already prepared an alternative to at least its financial aspects. John Maynard Keynes, a brilliant economist with a sharp tongue and a healthy disrespect for authority, believed that the reparations schemes in the treaty had the potential to create economic chaos on a global level. Without economic stability, he doubted whether the postwar world would be able to achieve political or social stability. Economic chaos would also play into the hands of the Bolsheviks and give credence to their attacks on the global capitalist system.

In April, Keynes had circulated a memo calling for an abandonment of the reparations approach. He feared that reparations would draw immense resources out of Germany, thus bankrupting it to no larger purpose. Like many other observers in Paris, Keynes worried that such a scheme would make it harder for Europe as a whole to recover because the German people would not have enough money to buy imports. Thus the reparations imposed on Germany would ultimately become self-defeating, bankrupting not just Germany but all of its prewar trade partners as well. They might also require Britain, France, and the United States to put resources back into the defeated countries in order to prevent revolution, famine, or epidemics from spreading, an eventuality that would prove both economically and politically perilous.

In place of reparations, Keynes proposed that the Allies jointly agree to reduce the war debts that they owed to one another as well as the debts that third-party states owed to them. With fewer debts burdening the European financial system, the British and French especially would have less need of reparations money from Germany with which to repay their own debts, most notably to the United States. Canceling reparations would also be more humane to the German people, sustain the capitalist system by getting people across the Continent back to work as quickly as possible, and be, in Keynes's own words, consistent with the spirit of the age. Canceling debts on which it was unlikely to collect in any case would also make the British government look generous in the eyes of potential allies and trading partners among the new states in Central and Eastern Europe.

Even with the cancellation of the redeemable debts in Central and Eastern Europe, the scheme should benefit Britain by reducing its own debt to the United States by an equivalent amount. The French, too, saw merit in the idea as a way out of their own debt problems. Forgiveness of debt could then be accompanied by a reduction of German reparations to an amount that the Germans could actually pay, thereby creating the basis, Keynes argued, for the rehabilitation of the European and global economies. With that rehabilitation would come strong markets for American exports to Europe. Everyone would thus gain from the plan, Europe would recover economically much more quickly, and the Continent would stabilize.

Keynes's scheme had much to recommend it, but it depended on the support of the United States, to which the British and French were deeply in debt. The Americans, however, were not sold on the idea of trading the guarantees of British and French debt for the promise of future growth in exports. American bankers loathed the idea of giving up their outstanding loans unless the American government was willing to make good their losses. Wilson worried that the federal government could not assume the debts of private banks unless the US Congress approved new legislation, an eventuality he thought highly unlikely. He also worried that the United States might end up paying the entire bill for the scheme without having any assurances in return of its success, a point that Keynes himself had to concede had validity.

The rejection of his plan to reduce war debts proved to be the final straw for a deeply unhappy Keynes. Announcing to Lloyd George on June 5 that he was leaving Paris or, as he put it, "slipping away from the scene of the nightmare," he returned to England disillusioned and bitter. He had already made up his mind to write the book for which he would become best known, *The Economic*

Consequences of the Peace. He was motivated, he told his mother, by his "deep and violent shame" at his own role in the conference. The treaty, he warned anyone who would listen, would produce an economic catastrophe.

Perhaps seeing for himself the damage the conference had done, Lloyd George announced his desire to revise some of the treaty terms in Germany's favor. But both Wilson and Clemenceau were unwilling to undo all of the work they had done, and some major issues like Fiume still needed their attention. The signing ceremony, moreover, had already been postponed twice. On June 16, the Allies closed all discussions with the Germans, acceding to only one of Brockdorff-Rantzau's points, a plebiscite for Upper Silesia. The Germans had three (later extended to seven) days to accept or the Allies threatened to renew hostilities. The French knew from intercepting German telegraph traffic that the German delegation was getting advice to reject the treaty based on how deeply unpopular it was among both the people and the government back home.

The treaty terms may have been humiliating to German pride, but the Germans had few realistic options. Foch may not have been able to assemble the forty infantry and five cavalry divisions that he claimed he had at his disposal, but Germany was certainly in no position to resume even a limited war. Influenza had taken a terrible toll on an underfed Germany, and the outbreak of a revolution or civil war seemed a genuine possibility. The Allied bridgeheads over the Rhine River and the internment of German warships after November 1918 made serious military resistance almost impossible. Still, few Allied officials looked forward to resuming the war or to the uncertain outcome of an invasion of even part of Germany.

The Allied leaders thus waited anxiously to see what the Germans would do. By mid-June they were fed up with one another, yet still deep in discussion about the future of Fiume and several other issues. The tense discussions over Fiume just before the treaty had been formally presented to them for their signature may well have distracted the Big Four from seeing the likely reactions of the Germans. In Germany itself, newspapers carried headlines claiming that the treaty would mean the end of the German nation and the enslavement of the German people.

For their part, the Allied leaders had as many reasons to be afraid of a German rejection as the Germans did. A June 16 meeting between the Big Four, Foch, and Foch's loyal deputy, Gen. Maxime Weygand, had ended badly. Foch admitted that he was not as optimistic as he had once been about the French army's ability to invade Germany and force the Germans to accept the treaty terms. He now judged the forty infantry divisions at his disposal too few to drive toward Berlin and secure Allied lines of communication on the way. When Foch proposed offering incentives to the southern German states to remain neutral in the event of an Allied invasion, the politicians grew suspicious about his interference in matters that they considered to be purely political.

For once, Wilson, Clemenceau, and Lloyd George were all in agreement: the plans of the generals did not conform to those of the politicians. Neither were they pleased with what they saw as Foch's and Weygand's borderline insubordination. Wilson warned his colleagues that the real danger to Europe might be in putting its future in the hands of generals like Weygand. Although it would be politically difficult to do so, Clemenceau and Lloyd George briefly considered replacing Foch with the far more cautious and obedient Henri-Philippe Pétain. Only Clemenceau's fear that changing commanders at so sensitive and volatile a moment would demonstrate weakness to the Germans prevented him from doing so.

Doubts and fear among them notwithstanding, the Big Four decided on a harsh line, hoping to compel a quick German decision to sign the treaty and end all doubt. In response to Brockdorff-Rantzau's continued requests for changes to the treaty, they released a statement accusing the Germans of committing "the greatest crime against humanity and freedom of peoples that any nation calling itself civilized has ever consciously committed." The statement, which a military officer delivered in person to Brockdorff-Rantzau's hotel room, reaffirmed that the responsibility for the war rested in Berlin and that the Germans must accept that responsibility by signing the treaty. The letter did not have the effect Clemenceau had sought. Instead of cowing Brockdorff-Rantzau into agreeing to sign, it led him to leave France and return to Germany determined to stop his nation from accepting the treaty in any form.

Back in Berlin, the German government had been debating, arguing, and disagreeing about its next move. The German army's senior leadership gave mixed signals, warning the government that it could not stop even a limited Allied attack and at the same time advising against signing such a humiliating and dishonorable treaty. The highly respected Gen. Wilhelm Groener warned that if the Allies resumed hostilities in the west, Poland might invade from the east to take more German land than the treaty had granted to it. He also warned of the possibility of a Bolshevik uprising inside Germany. He rejected as a utopian fantasy any notion that the German people might rise up in arms as they had done a century earlier to help defeat Napoleon. Still, he closed his memorandum to the government by telling them that notwithstanding the dire circumstances Germany faced, he preferred an honorable defeat to a dishonorable peace.

In the end, the advice of the military to the civilian government was less clear and less helpful than the latter might have wanted. An invasion might also lead, as Foch had indeed planned, to the breaking of the southern German states from the northern ones or the detachment of the Rhineland. Such an eventuality would undo the great triumph of modern German history, its unification in the nineteenth century under Prussian leadership. The only real hope

To bed, sick of life

for Germany seemed to rest in the possibility that the Allies were bluffing and would back down rather than resume the war. Unwilling to believe in that possibility enough to bet their nation's future on it and still deadlocked, the German cabinet resigned on June 20 rather than vote in favor of accepting the treaty. Gustav Noske, the defense minister, wryly remarked that the fifteen members of that cabinet were heroes for their resignations but that Germany did not need any more heroes.

Allied troops on the Rhine prepared for the possibility that the Germans might refuse to sign and then call on even more of their sons to become heroes. Foch again presented his plan, this time to a larger assemblage of Allied military and political officials. Clemenceau and Weygand did not speak to one another and, perhaps as a warning to Foch, the prime minster had invited Pétain, Foch's only obvious potential successor, to the meeting as well. Gen. Sir William Robertson, speaking for the British, and Gen. Tasker H. Bliss, speaking for the Americans, both threw cold water on Foch's plans, noting how much their two armies had demobilized since November. Robertson thought that the only chance of success would come from asking the Poles and the Czechs to declare war on Germany, with promises of even more German territory as their reward. Pétain doubted even that would prove decisive. As was typical of his strategic assessments, Pétain was pessimistic and predicted a new war against a Germany that would find more than a million men to resist an Allied invasion. The meeting ended with the decision to approach the southern German states about separate peaces if the Berlin government did not sign, notwithstanding the common understanding that such agreements would undo all of the months of work on the treaty.

A genuine crisis seemed to be at hand. The situation around June 20 should remind us how thin the line can be between history as it happened and history as it might have happened. Only the decision by Provisional President Friedrich Ebert to remain in office avoided a complete catastrophe in the wake of the resignation of the Philipp Scheidemann cabinet. As a socialist and Germany's first popularly elected head of state, he had the authority with the left to form a new cabinet. Although he, too, hated the terms that the Treaty of Versailles imposed, he saw no point in risking a new war that could not materially improve Germany's chances at obtaining a better peace. When the Allies warned that it would not give Germany any more time to consider the treaty, Ebert asked the army for a final judgment. The generals recommended signing, even as a number of its leaders had already begun to think of ways to get around many of the treaty's terms.

Mass demonstrations appeared across Germany in opposition to the proposed treaty's terms as reported, more or less accurately, by the German press. Notably, those demonstrations included the southern German states, underscoring the difficulties the Allies would have in getting them to sign separate treaties. In Scotland's Scapa Flow, bored and demoralized German sailors sitting on their surrendered ships heard the news that the treaty would turn those ships over to the British. Rather than see their ships be given over to the enemy, they scuttled fifteen of them. In the ensuing chaos, British troops killed nine German soldiers and wounded a further sixteen. In Berlin, Germans praised the scuttlings and celebrated the dead sailors as heroes.

The new German cabinet, headed by the labor minister Gustav Bauer, agreed to sign the treaty notwithstanding its members' opposition to its terms and to Allied unwillingness to revise the articles on war guilt. Bauer announced to the National Assembly that his cabinet did not seek ambition or power. Rather, he told them, "it is our damned duty to save what can be saved." A somber assembly, warned once again by the army that it could not stop an Allied invasion, voted in favor of signing by 237 to 138, although it urged the Allies to consider a revision of the clauses of German guilt. The line between war, peace, and revolution might thus have been quite thin indeed, certainly a great deal thinner than we often appreciate today. Had the Bauer cabinet decided on a showdown, had the German army encouraged the government to resist, or had the Germans somehow gotten wind of the doubts and fears among the Big Four in Paris, then it is easy to imagine another outcome.

Clemenceau returned from a weekend away to hear both the bad news from Scapa Flow and the good news that the new German government would, in fact, sign the treaty. Neither one put him in much of a mood for revising the treaty's terms or for planning an elaborate and grandiose ceremony. Privately, he regretted the decision to allow the British to send the German fleet to Scapa Flow, believing that they would take its scuttling almost as a personal affront. The British were, in fact, quite angry, only adding to the sour mood in Paris. Even Wilson's attitude turned more forceful. Consequently, the Big Four turned down the Bauer cabinet's final suggestion for a delay of the signing ceremony. The anger inside Germany was palpable. On June 23, a group of German students had seized the French flags captured in 1871 that the treaty demanded be returned to the French. The students had taken them to a statue of Frederick the Great and burned them while singing "Deutschland über Alles." "They are mocking us," Foch wrote to his wife. "All of Europe is a complete mess. Such is the work of Clemenceau."

As late as the night of June 23, Lloyd George still feared that the Germans would not sign. An angry Foch went to his forward headquarters on the Rhine River to be with his troops in the event of a resumption of hostilities. Finally, at six thirty that evening the German government informed Foch of its decision to sign the treaty as written. Foch then transmitted the news to the Big Four. Within thirty minutes the news was making its way through the streets of Paris. The war was soon to be truly and officially over.

Given all the tension, it was probably inevitable that the celebrations and the signing ceremony itself struck participants as anticlimactic and even a bit morose. Clemenceau insisted on holding the ceremony in the Hall of Mirrors of Versailles on June 28, at least symbolically closing the chapter in European history that had begun in the same room in 1871 and giving the treaty the name it has carried ever since. Workers hurried to get the room ready and to find a way to accommodate as many people as they could for the ceremony itself. The United States, Great Britain, France, Italy, and Japan each received sixty places in the gallery. Journalists, minor officials, and interested citizens scrambled to buy tickets or bribe porters to allow them into adjacent rooms so they could at least hear the moment for themselves.

The Germans did not name their official representatives until the last minute; rumors going around Paris said that no Germans could be found who were willing to put their names on such a humiliating treaty. Eventually, the Bauer cabinet named two men as signatories, Herman Müller, a socialist who had recently been named foreign minister, and the new minister for the colonies, Johannes Bell of the Catholic Centre Party. That Bell's first act in his new job would be to sign away the very colonies for which he had just assumed responsibility did not escape the notice of people in Berlin. He had, in fact, also been given the portfolio for the ministry of transport on the assumption that the colonial office would itself not long survive.

The ceremony was brief and, to many eyes, not worthy of the occasion. Clemenceau said little, merely ordering that the Germans be brought into the gallery. They entered less as visiting dignitaries than, as Headlam-Morley described them, prisoners about to hear their sentences. Once they had signed, Clemenceau closed the ceremonies with as little fanfare as he had opened them. They had lasted just fifty minutes in all, most of that time taken up by the parade of Allied representatives who had to sign. The foreign minister of Uruguay was the last to do so. Within hours, Woodrow Wilson had left Paris, never to see France again. Lloyd George was back in London the next day.

Almost no one walked away impressed by the ceremonies. Great Britain's Harold Nicolson went back to his hotel room and wrote in his diary, "To bed, sick of life." Headlam-Morley lamented that the ceremony did not produce a sense of reconciliation but rather underscored the theme of revenge and embittered the Germans, who, he noted, would not take their humiliation lying down. Tasker H. Bliss wrote, "What a wretched mess it all is!" but thought that the German signing at least postponed the risk of war or revolution "here, there, and everywhere" long enough to make Europe safe for his wife to come visit him. Noticeable by their absence were Foch, Pétain, and most of the other senior French military leaders, who had stayed away as a silent protest against a treaty that they believed would not protect France's essential security needs. The Allies had Germany's signature and could put the treaty into action, but even as the ink was drying, the doubts were building, as events from Berlin to Beijing were already proving.

Chapter 6
War to end war?

Stuyvesant Van Veen's 1932 painting *Peace Conference* depicts anonymous statesmen in the front of an auditorium delivering a speech to which no one is really listening while rivers of blood pour down the aisles. Soldiers ignore the words of the politicians in front of them while they continue to fight. The words "War to End War" appear in red letters and form the source of the river of blood that flows down toward the speakers. In the background of the painting are airplanes, machine guns, dead men impaled on barbed wire, and artillery pieces, all symbols of the futility and costs of the war. They are also reminders of the wars that continued to rage even while the peace conference was ongoing as well as the bloody conflicts that the conference left behind.

The rivers of blood were real enough even as early as the spring of 1919, although it is unfair to place all of the blame for them on the flaws in the treaty. Still, the world that the Treaty of Versailles left behind looked anything but peaceful. Even as the ceremonies at Versailles were taking place, the Russian Civil War was threatening to engulf Europe in a war of ideologies. Anti-communist White forces under Anton Denikin drove the Bolshevik Red forces out of the Caucasus and were moving toward Kiev. Just a week before the signing ceremony in Versailles, White general Peter Wrangel recaptured the strategic city of Tsaritsyn (today Volgograd). But if the success of the Whites led some in the West to hope for a rapid defeat of the Bolsheviks and an end to the threat that they posed to Continental stability, they were soon to be disappointed. Within a few weeks, the Red armies, competently led by Gen. Mikhail Tukhachevski, had driven the Whites out of central Ukraine, secured Kiev, and pushed Wrangel's army all the way to the Black Sea. Within a few years, Tsaritsyn would be renamed Stalingrad in recognition both of the importance of the city in the Russian Civil War and the role that Josef Stalin himself had played there. At the time, the conflict in Russia terrified leaders in the West, while also inspiring communists in Hungary, Germany, and elsewhere.

A White victory would certainly not have solved all of Russia's myriad problems, but a Red victory was a nightmare for the statesmen of the Paris Peace Conference. The Reds offered a far different explanation of the world war from that being proposed by the conservative statesmen of the West. The Bolsheviks believed that the war had resulted from a morally bankrupt capitalist competition for empires, markets, and natural resources. The Treaty of Versailles itself seemed to prove the case, concentrating power as it did in the capitalist states while subjugating much of the former Ottoman and German empires and forcing them to participate in the capitalist world order. The only way to avoid the calamity of a global capitalist takeover, the Reds argued, was to prepare for, and if necessary fight, a class-based war across Europe and perhaps the world.

Most immediately, the Bolsheviks posed a threat to the new Poland as the two states disputed the borders that the peace process had set in Eastern Europe. Although they had drawn Poland's new borders in Paris, the British, French, and Americans could do little to ensure that the Soviets, or for that matter the Germans, would respect them. For that reason, French leaders like Gens. Ferdinand Foch and Maxime Weygand wanted France and Britain to provide equipment and technical assistance to the new Polish army so that it could better defend itself. A strong Poland, they hoped, would balance the power of Germany and the Soviet Union while providing France with a grateful ally in Eastern Europe. Other Western officials either wanted to stay out of the dispute or, in some cases, blamed the Poles for trying to expand their borders while the Russians were distracted by their civil war. Polish forces did indeed drive east, capturing territory that was supposed to become part of the new states of Lithuania and Ukraine. These moves gave Poland enemies on all sides of its already indefensible borders. Less than a year after the signing of the Treaty of Versailles, the Soviet Union and Poland were at war.

European conservatives worried that a Soviet victory in that war would destroy an already fragile Poland, destabilize central Europe, and bring a Bolshevik government up to the German border. Stopping the Soviet Union as far east as possible therefore became a priority of the highest order. Initial Soviet success on the battlefield only added to the climate of fear. Weygand went to Warsaw to help the Poles plan and prepare a counterattack (one of his subordinate officers was a young Charles de Gaulle), partly with Polish veterans of the Allied armies of the First World War formed into a French-led "Blue Army." In August 1920, Polish forces won a critical victory outside Warsaw that contemporaries compared to Charles Martel's victory over the Moors in 732. Whereas Martel had stopped a Moorish threat to Europe from the south, the Poles had stopped a communist one from the east.

There was thus great sympathy and gratitude in the west toward the Poles, although sympathy and gratitude had their limits. Neither France nor Great Britain had any desire to risk an extension of the brewing war in the east, although they did seek to form alliances with a strong Poland, Czechoslovakia, and Romania. They therefore supported Poland's extensive land claims against the Soviet Union in the 1921 Treaty of Riga even at the risk of future tensions with the Soviets. That treaty produced the so-called Riga Line, which gave Poland fifty thousand more square miles of

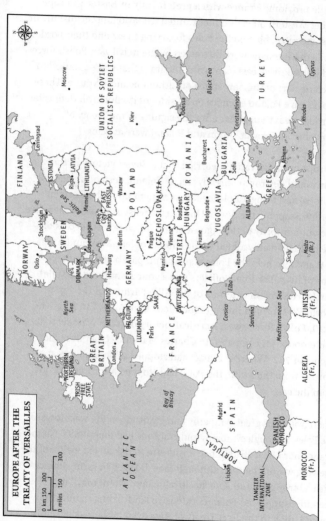

10. **The Big Four tried to replace Europe's imperial boundaries with ones based more on nationality. Doing so, however, created thorny security and economic problems for the new states.**

Russian, Lithuanian, and Ukrainian territory than the Paris Peace Conference had promised.

Although its victory over the Soviet Union made Poland larger and stronger, France and Britain reacted coolly to the Treaty of Riga, in large part because it overturned the settlements of Paris by force. The borders of Poland thus became one of the first major provisions of the Paris Peace Conference revealed as unenforceable. Instead of being negotiated with or arbitrated by the League of Nations, the new Polish border had been determined by brute force. It therefore struck most Europeans as a symbol of the futility of the very concepts that had ostensibly informed the Treaty of Versailles. Russians, Ukrainians, and Lithuanians reacted with bitter anger at Poland's land grabs, as well as at France and Britain for their support of the Poles. As even many Polish officials recognized, the Treaty of Riga was a Pyrrhic victory, giving Poland land (much of it not inhabited by ethnic Poles) at the cost of bitter enmity from the country's new neighbors. It also created a border with the Soviet Union that had few natural defenses and gave the pariah states of Germany and the Soviet Union a common grievance.

The Polish case was symbolic of larger problems of enforcing the terms of the treaty. The Treaty of Versailles made enormous demands for reparations from Germany that even many of the treaty's own authors believed to be unreasonable. When the Germans predictably failed to make their scheduled payment of 20 billion marks in 1921 the Allies faced a serious political dilemma. To try to enforce the terms as written in Paris would look heavy-handed, especially as feelings about the treaty had grown more critical and attitudes toward the Germans had warmed somewhat since the end of the war. Pulling so much money out of Germany might also, as Keynes had warned, be both self-defeating and destabilizing because the European economy could not fully recover until Germany became a major producer and purchaser once again. Still, to not enforce the reparations demands would also set a poor precedent and would anger those people, especially in France, who accused the Germans of intentionally dragging their feet on making good the payments they had, however reluctantly, agreed to honor.

The French also needed German reparations payments in order to pay back the debts they themselves owed, especially to American banks. The issue was both a financial one and a political one. America's strict refusal to forgive or renegotiate France's enormous debts led to a wave of anti-American sentiment in France, only made worse by American unwillingness to join the very League of Nations it had so forcefully sponsored. French newspapers were soon running cartoons showing the United States as an ungrateful Shylock, unwilling to accept the blood France had spilled in the common quest for victory as payment on the loans. The play *Les Américains chez nous* (1920), by the Académie Française's noted playwright Eugène Brieux, played on these tensions. It depicts a French father and daughter of the old-fashioned landed aristocracy living in a simple manor house in Burgundy. When the house catches fire, modern, sophisticated American firemen put out the blaze, then move right in, taking the lord's bedroom as their own.

Mutual allegations of ingratitude aside, as long as the Americans insisted on getting their money, France needed German reparations. Without reparations, the French would see their national wealth go to their erstwhile American allies in the form of debt payments while Germany retained its own resources by evading its treaty obligations. British willingness to be lenient to the Germans in order to encourage the Germans to once again become consumers of British goods only exacerbated the problem. France, ostensibly the war's winner, would grow poorer from the peace settlement, while Germany would grow relatively wealthier. Strikes and demonstrations on a huge scale had already shown the fragility of the French economy as it struggled to recover from the war's enormous dislocations. No French government could long survive if it could not find a way out of the conundrum that the reparations crisis posed, yet the French were receiving no diplomatic or military help from either the Americans or the British.

When in January 1923 Germany defaulted on promised monthly coal shipments for the thirty-fourth time in three years, French prime minister Raymond Poincaré, with Belgian support, decided to send troops into the Saar and Ruhr districts. German miners, unwilling to work if the fruits of their labor simply went to their recent enemies, went on strike. Poincaré tried to bring in French miners to keep the mines operating, but the scheme was deeply unpopular and cost the French government far more money than it gained from the production of coal. The French also put down German protests and strikes with violence, killing 130 Germans and turning international opinion decidedly anti-French. Runaway inflation and a lack of confidence in the strength of the French franc created a genuine crisis, especially as the Germans appeared for the first time since well before 1914 as sympathetic victims. Anxious to see the situation calm down as quickly as possible, neither the United States nor Great Britain backed French efforts, revealing once and for all to French leaders that they could not count on help from their wartime allies.

A new round of Franco-German hostilities certainly seemed to be one possible outcome of the Ruhr crisis. Right-wing groups pledged to resort to violence rather than see Germany humiliated once again. Nationalists called for a *levée en masse* at the height of the Ruhr crisis to restore the honor of Germany and to show that Germans could defend their nation's interests in defeat every bit as well as the French had defended theirs at the end of the Franco-Prussian War. Others pointed to the rising of the Prussian people against Napoleon in 1814 as a model. The Ruhr and Saar occupations may have allowed France to recoup some of the money Germany owed, but the whole situation proved to be an economic, political, and public relations disaster. An international agreement in the form of the American-led Dawes Plan reduced the total amount of money Germany owed to France, but not the amount France owed to the United States. French conservatives were outraged at Germany's ability to essentially abrogate one of the centerpieces of the Treaty of Versailles by simply refusing to comply with it.

Historians continue to debate whether or not the Ruhr crisis sparked the hyperinflation that hit Germany soon thereafter, but whether causation or correlation, the two events became linked in the minds of people across the Continent, and Poincaré's cabinet took much of the blame. For their part, French leaders realized how limited their powers of enforcement over the Treaty of Versailles really were, as well as how unreliable their former allies were proving to be. French voters expressed their displeasure, voting out Poincaré's center-right government and voting in a left-leaning cabinet that had promised a more conciliatory attitude toward the Germans.

The Saar crisis effectively ended attempts to enforce the Treaty of Versailles as written. By then, the American Senate had already rejected it, the Poles had changed their border with the Soviet Union by force, and Germany had refused to mine coal bound for France. The treaty had in a few short months become something far different from what its framers had designed. Those framers were themselves out of the picture and largely discredited. Georges Clemenceau left office in January 1920 and lost his bid for the French presidency in humiliating fashion to a relatively unknown challenger. That election dealt with many issues, but the French treated it as a kind of referendum on the Treaty of Versailles, and Clemenceau had clearly lost it. By that time Woodrow Wilson had been incapacitated by strokes. The treaty thus had few champions left to plead its case.

The governments of Western Europe soon changed tack from enforcement of the treaty to a more general policy of rapprochement. This approach had some notable successes, mostly in the Treaty of Locarno in 1925 that brought Germany into the League of Nations, reaffirmed the borders of Western Europe, removed French troops from their zones of occupation in the Rhineland, and, to Poland's horror, left open the possibility of Germany adjusting its borders in the east. Critics complained that Germany had gained a great deal without having to give up anything significant, but the so-called Spirit of Locarno was popular across the Continent because it offered some sliver of hope to a war-weary region for the first time in more than a decade. Its German and French negotiators shared the 1926 Nobel Peace Prize, in large part for showing an alternative path to European stability than the Treaty of Versailles, which looked even worse from half a decade's remove than it had in 1919. Within a few more years, Van Veen's painting would reveal how much lower the reputation of the treaty had sunk.

The treaty scarcely had a better history outside Europe. Beijing, Shanghai, and much of the rest of China had been in a state of intellectual and political ferment since the Revolution of 1911 had deposed the centuries-old system of dynasties. In its place had come not democracy and freedom but a series of warlords competing with one another to take over the reins of power. Some of those warlords looked to work with Japan; they were willing to form alliances with a foreign enemy in order to solidify their political position at home.

The First World War had starkly revealed both China's weakness and Japan's strength. That strength had led the British, especially, to support the acquisitive sights Japan had set on China, as articulated in the Twenty-One Demands Japan imposed on the Chinese government in 1915. Idealistic Chinese students and young intellectuals had formed movements such as the influential New Youth Movement that hoped to build China's future on democracy, science, and individual rights. They also hoped that Wilsonian principles of national self-determination would help them to regain full control of Chinese territory and remove the humiliating legal and economic privileges that foreigners enjoyed in China as well as economic and political concessions like those included in the Twenty-One Demands.

The New Youth Movement's leaders had put great faith in Woodrow Wilson, the Fourteen Points, and the Paris Peace Conference as ways to protect them from foreign acquisitiveness. That faith turned to anger and disillusion when, in early May 1919, news reached China that the Big Three had decided to give economic control of the Shandong Peninsula to Japan. Thousands of protesters marched through the streets of Beijing on May 4, protesting Japanese businesses, expressing their anger at the Western leaders in Paris, and burning down the house of a prominent Chinese politician with ties to Japan. Calls for a full boycott of Western and Japanese goods soon followed, as did a wave of strikes in Shanghai, Wuhan, and other Chinese cities.

The demonstrations had important repercussions, even if the Chinese government quickly put a stop to most of them. On June 10, several key Chinese officials resigned their positions in protest of the Shandong decision, leaving Chinese diplomats in Paris unsure of whether Beijing wanted them to sign the treaty or not. Chinese students living in France answered that question for them by surrounding their hotel and demanding that they refuse to sign the treaty unless the Big Three reversed their decision and gave Shandong to China. Unhappy with the treaty themselves, and having no orders from Beijing to sign, the Chinese delegates decided to boycott the ceremony.

Not having China present among the signatories was another of the bad tastes that the signing ceremony left behind. British diplomat Sir James Headlam-Morley and American general Tasker H. Bliss were among the senior officials who sympathized with the Chinese and thought they had been correct to refuse to put their names on a treaty so humiliating to their country. The Shandong decision was deeply unpopular not only among the

Chinese, but also among diplomats in Paris who recognized just how badly it undermined the very principles upon which they were trying to rebuild the world. Headlam-Morley worried about the ramifications of China's noninvolvement in that new world order. Chinese anger at the West, as well as the West's acquiescence in Japan's power grab, would inevitably lead to an increase in Japanese strength, a development that worried both the Europeans and the Americans. It also, Headlam-Morley feared, set up the dangerous possibility of the creation of a bloc of anti–League of Nations states led by an alliance between Germany, the Soviet Union, and China. Neither option augured well for the West or for stability in East Asia.

The Americans, too, were worried about the growth of Japanese power, but Wilson scarcely had time to think about Asia. First he had to find a way to get the US Senate to approve the Treaty of Versailles and its most controversial provision, the Covenant of the League of Nations. The battle to do so proved to be one of the most arduous, partisan, and acrimonious debates in the history of American politics. In the end it may well have led Wilson to suffer the strokes that incapacitated him, destroyed the remainder of his presidency, and muddled his legacy.

The debate over the League had myriad dimensions, both international and domestic. The US Constitution is surprisingly vague on matters of foreign policy. As they did on so many other occasions, the authors of that document sought to divide power. In this case, they authorized the president to negotiate treaties but required the Senate to approve them by a two-thirds majority before they became law. American presidents have wrestled with the Senate ever since over how to make foreign policy within those parameters. Never, however, had there been a treaty as complex and wide-ranging as the one that Wilson had negotiated in Paris. Nor had there been a treaty that might force the United States to participate in far-flung international crises without the approval of its elected officials. While Wilson was negotiating on the nation's behalf in Paris, senators of both parties back in Washington worried that the president had gone too far in committing the United States without the proper consultation of the legislature. They were determined to exercise what they believed was their constitutional obligation to rein in presidential excess.

By most accounts, the treaty and American participation in the League of Nations had broad public support. In the Senate, however, opinions were not quite so favorable. A large bloc of senators supported ratification of the treaty, but two sizable groups threatened to prevent the formation of the required two-thirds majority needed to make it law. One group, the Reservationists, did not oppose the treaty per se, but they wanted to see modifications made, especially language that they feared could compel the United States to take part in military operations overseas if the League of Nations so decided. As the Reservationists noted, the Constitution gave the power to make war to the Senate, not to an international body based in Geneva. Some Reservationists also feared that the many Latin American states could join together to convince the League to rewrite the guarantees built into the Treaty of Versailles that explicitly protected American rights in Latin America. They included the Monroe Doctrine and the Platt Amendment, which guaranteed American rights to intervene in Cuba. Many of those same senators had been supporters of American intervention into Mexico in 1916 in response to Pancho Villa's raid into New Mexico, and they worried that the League could make such interventions more difficult or even lead other states to declare war on the United States in response.

A smaller group, soon to be known as the Irreconcilables, opposed the treaty on fundamental philosophical and ideological grounds. They argued that both American national security and global stability were far better served by America retaining full sovereignty and not being bound in any way by the dictates of an international organization like the League. Some of them were prewar Progressives who mistrusted American interventions overseas and feared that the League would make such interventions more, not less, common. Others shared Wilson's general goal of preventing future conflict but did not have faith in the League to be the instrument to achieve it.

One of their spokesmen, Elihu Root, a former presidential candidate and former secretary of both the war and state departments, fired the first major salvo in the debate while Wilson was still in Paris. Root had won the Nobel Peace Prize for his ideas on binding arbitration in world politics. He therefore had the experience and gravitas to challenge the president on his foreign policy views. On June 21, Root wrote an open letter in the American press blasting the League of Nations and the "vast and incalculable obligation" it would force on the United States to fight wars not necessarily of its choosing. Root and those who thought like him worried that, far from ensuring peace, the League had the potential to turn every small diplomatic conflict in the world into a global war. Small nations might also be able to use the League to co-opt American power to their own strategic ends. Among those who agreed with Root was the powerful and eloquent chairman of the Senate Foreign Relations Committee, Massachusetts senator Henry Cabot Lodge. Lodge believed that America was the world's best hope and feared that the League could fritter away American power. To make matters worse, the personal hatred between Lodge and Wilson had only deepened.

Wilson responded to Root's letter and the building opposition to the League by holding a press conference in Paris the day before the signing ceremony. It was the only press conference Wilson gave while in Europe. He laid out a logical and rational case for the League and may well have expected that the statement, plus the high level of support he believed to exist among the American people, would suffice to get the two-thirds of senators needed for ratification. But in his first major address in Washington on July 10, he had angered League opponents by not even addressing their criticisms and belittling their views. Wilson's arrogance and inflexibility energized his rivals to organize opposition to the treaty.

Tired of fighting with the Senate, Wilson went on a grueling speaking tour, hoping to go directly to the American people, whom he believed to be on his side. Wilson counted on the American public being more in favor of the League than their elected officials, many of whom faced reelection in 1920. He hoped the voters would pressure their senators to accept the treaty and the League. He had reason to believe that his appraisal of the mood of the American people was right, but he also knew that his health was declining. Although the details remain far from clear, he appears to have suffered from a series of small strokes leading to a much larger one in late September 1919 in Pueblo, Colorado, that forced him to return to Washington, where he had yet another stroke. In mid-November, a group of senators made one more attempt to negotiate a compromise, but Wilson either would not or could not receive them. The Treaty of Versailles and the League of Nations were dead in the United States, although their supporters did try to keep the idea alive until March 1920.

Wilson's successor, Warren Harding, did not even answer letters or formal inquiries from League officials. Harding's approach to the League of Nations was symbolic of the general approach to the Versailles settlement. Even before its signing, the treaty had become an easy punching bag, blamed for almost all of the evils that followed from a terrible, destructive war that had demolished an old order without leaving anything tangible in its wake. A century later, it remains difficult to describe the treaty or the wider process of making peace at the end of the First World War as a success, in part because we know about the greater cataclysms that Europe was destined to endure two short decades later. Even on its own terms, however, the treaty looked bad to contemporaries and looks little better with the passage of time. Built on far too many narrow compromises and a flawed vision of a world still governed by a small number of great powers, it failed to reflect or take into account the massive changes that the war had unleashed.

Still, it need not have happened that way. The Treaty of Versailles's terms were no harsher in broad outline than those the Germans had imposed on Romania and Russia, and certainly no harsher than those that Germany was prepared to impose on Britain and France if it had won. Moreover, the 1920s spirit of Locarno and even more idealistic measures like the Kellogg-Briand Pact (1928) that outlawed war as an instrument of resolving international disputes showed that at least some influential Europeans (perhaps a majority) were interested in finding a more peaceful way forward. Even the now completely discredited strategy of appeasement had as one of its main, if misguided, aims the amelioration of some of the worst aspects of the Treaty of Versailles in the hopes of making the Germans accept its basic provisions.

In one sense, the history of the Treaty of Versailles was not so different from others produced at the end of the First World War. Like the Treaties of Brest-Litovsk, Bucharest, and Sèvres, they did not endure because the circumstances surrounding their birth quickly changed. What seemed to make diplomatic sense in November 1918 no longer fit into the world of June 1919. The months of willful lies about battlefield victory and the treachery of domestic enemies that the German leadership fed to its people at the end of a bloody and futile struggle surely poisoned any remote chance of long-term success that the treaty might have had, as did the failure of the Allies to at least acknowledge that the Germans believed themselves to have entered into a negotiation based on Wilson's Fourteen Points. What the Germans got instead was a document they could neither influence nor adequately explain to their own people.

Still, had the global economy held together reasonably well in the postwar period, or had the German political system been better able to withstand the turmoil the Nazis presented, then perhaps the Treaty of Versailles would have a better reputation today. It might have faded away gradually until few diplomats paid it any sustained attention. British and French politicians certainly showed a willingness to reform many of the treaty's provisions. It is unlikely that the German right would ever have accepted the validity of the Versailles *Diktat*, but perhaps over time it would have lost some of its power to mobilize and catalyze German anger. It is also possible that an active and productive American role in the League of Nations and the post-Versailles settlement could have been a positive force for global stability. In this sense, the resistance of a group of irreconcilable senators may have had a greater impact on global security than even they envisioned.

The treaty, and the Paris Peace Conference that produced it, really had two lives. One involved the actual policies, borders, and institutions that the treaty created. Scholars have recently been a bit kinder to some of these changes, most notably the concept of international organizations like the League of Nations. If it did not create the peaceful world that some had hoped that it might, the League at the very least created a precedent for dealing cooperatively, if not always successfully, with a variety of crises. It also helped to establish international norms for everything from child labor regulations to industrial standardization. Despite America's rejection of these innovations in the postwar years and despite the dominance of them by the British and French, the League nevertheless looks better at a century's remove than it did in its own day.

The treaty's second life is the symbolic role it has played through history. To Germans of the interwar period, it was a symbol of their defeat, and one that their misbegotten belief in their own battlefield success rendered all the more impossible to accept. To Americans, it came to symbolize all that they sought to separate themselves from in Europe and its empires. This did not mean that Americans sought no role in the interwar years. "Isolationism" to Americans of the 1920s meant not ignoring the outside world but dealing with it on their own terms, unconstrained by alliances or international organizations. To many British and French analysts, especially on the left and in the center, the treaty revealed the naked imperialism and power grabs that it seemed to many must have been the real purpose of the war all along.

The Treaty of Versailles empowered a wide variety of narratives developed by people frustrated by the wreckage of the First World War and the inability of the victorious diplomats to do anything meaningful about it. Instead, they had written a document that punished the German people for the actions of a regime that was now discredited and out of power. The deposed kaiser himself sat in a comfortable exile in Holland, immune from prosecution and, by the time of his second marriage in 1922, an object of a certain kind of nostalgia for a prewar world long gone by that looked to many people a great deal kinder and more stable than the one that replaced it.

In the end, it remains hard to see how any treaty could have healed the wounds of 1914–18. That war may have begun because of the decisions of a small group of elites, but it had quickly become a classic peoples' war, unleashing the energies of a continent and transforming societies in unimagined ways. The Treaty of Versailles tried to put the elites back in charge and at least attempt to calm the passions the war had unleashed. Many people at the conference knew that no treaty could possibly achieve that end. They worried about the new hatreds and passions that the end of the war would leave behind. They were right to worry, and we know now how long those embers would retain the ability to cause major fires. It is perhaps asking too much to have expected the men of 1919 to have prevented them all, but it is also unavoidable to conclude that their work did as much harm as good.

As the victorious powers of 1945 gathered at Potsdam to end the Second World War, they all stated that they wanted to reject the Paris Peace Conference as a model. There would be no long-term schedule of reparations, no listening to the pleas of delegations from across the globe, and no final, inflexible document to bind the next generation of diplomats. That the men of 1945 saw fit to state so openly their rejection of the work of the men of 1919 speaks volumes about the reputation of the Treaty of Versailles and its place in the history of peacemaking.

References

Preface

William Westermann quotations come from his papers at Columbia
University Rare Books and Manuscript Library, MS #1322, box 5,
p. 102.

William Bullitt quotation is from Godfrey Hodgson, *Woodrow Wilson's
Right Hand: The Life of Colonel Edward M. House* (New Haven:
Yale University Press, 2006), p. 177.

Chapter 1: From war to armistice to peace conference

John Pershing quoted in Bullitt Lowry, *Armistice 1918* (Kent, OH:
Kent State University Press, 1996), p. 96.

Lloyd George's comment on Foch is from Jere Clemens King, *Foch
Versus Clemenceau* (Cambridge, MA: Harvard University Press,
1960), p. 26.

Foch to Clemenceau from *Times of London*, November 9, 1920.

The "squeeze the pips" comment comes from Keith Grieves, *Sir Eric
Geddes: Business and Government in War and Peace* (Manchester:
Manchester University Press, 1989), p. 72.

Paul Cambon's quotation is from Alan Sharp, "James Headlam-
Morley: Creating International History," *Diplomacy and Statecraft*
9, no. 3 (Fall 1988): pp. 266–283.

Harold Nicolson's quotation is from his *Peacemaking, 1919* (London:
University Paperbacks, 1964), p. 32.

Chapter 2: The big three (or maybe four)

Wilson quoted in John Milton Cooper, *Reconsidering Woodrow Wilson* (Baltimore: Johns Hopkins University Press, 2008), p. 13.

Chapter 3: Ideals versus interests

Wilson to the Inquiry from John Milton Cooper, *Breaking the Heart of the World: Woodrow Wilson and the Fight for the League of Nations* (Cambridge: Cambridge University Press, 2001), p. 45.

Wilson to Creel is quoted in George Herring, *From Colony to Superpower: US Foreign Relations Since 1776* (New York: Oxford University Press, 2008), p. 414.

British diplomat, from Margaret Macmillan, *Paris 1919: Six Months That Changed the World* (New York: Random House, 2003), p. 3.

For Engels, see Manfred Boemke, Roger Chickering, and Stig Förster, *Anticipating Total War* (Cambridge: Cambridge University Press, 1999), p. 347.

Bliss quotations are from Frederick Palmer, *Bliss, Peacemaker* (New York: Dodd, Mead, 1934), pp. 375 and 390.

Sonnino is quoted in Margaret Macmillan, *Paris 1919: Six Months That Changed the World* (New York: Random House, 2003), p. 285.

Chapter 4: Drafting the treaty

James Headlam-Morley quotation is from his *A Memoir of the Paris Peace Conference* (London: Methuen, 1972), p. 5.

Donald Moggridge, *Maynard Keynes: An Economist's Biography* (London: Routledge, 1992), p. 311.

Chapter 5: To bed, sick of life

James Headlam-Morley quotation is from his *A Memoir of the Paris Peace Conference* (London: Methuen, 1972), p. 118.

Clemenceau is quoted in Gregor Dallas, *At the Heart of a Tiger* (London: Macmillan, 1993), p. 577.

Bliss quotation from letter to his wife, January 14, 1919 in Bliss Papers, box 22, folder 12, United States Army Heritage and Education Center, Carlisle, Pennsylvania.

Wilson on the Germans is from William Bottom and Dejun Kong, "The Casual Cruelty of Our Prejudices," *Journal of the History of the Behavioral Sciences* 48, no. 4 (Sept. 2012): pp. 363–394.

Keynes is quoted in Robert Skidelsky, *Keynes, 1883–1946* (London: Penguin, 2005), p. 231.

The Allied statement following Brockdorff-Rantzau's speech is in Isabel Hull, *A Scrap of Paper* (Ithaca: Cornell University Press, 2014), p. 10.

Bauer is cited in Regierungsbildung und Annahme des Versailler Vertrags, http://www.bundesarchiv.de/aktenreichskanzlei/ 1919-1933/0000/bau/bau1p/kap1_1/para2_2.html.

Foch is cited in Jean Autin, *Foch* (Paris: Perrin, 1987), p. 265.

Nicolson's quotation comes from his *Peacemaking, 1919* (London: University Paperbacks, 1964), p. 371.

Bliss's quotation is from Frederick Palmer, *Bliss, Peacemaker* (New York: Dodd, Mead, 1934), p. 129.

Chapter 6: War to end war?

Root is quoted in his *League of Nations: Letters to Henry Cabot Lodge* (Washington, DC: Government Printing Office, 1919), p. 19.

Further reading

Good general introductions to the Paris Peace Conference include Margaret Macmillan, *Paris 1919: Six Months That Changed the World* (New York: Random House, 2003), and Alan Sharp, *The Versailles Settlement* (London: Palgrave Macmillan, 2008). David Fromkin, *A Peace to End All Peace: Creating the Modern Middle East, 1914–1922* (New York: Holt, 2009); Erez Manela, *The Wilsonian Moment: Self-Determination and the International Origins of Anti-Colonial Nationalism* (New York: Oxford University Press, 2007); John Milton Cooper, *Breaking the Heart of the World: Woodrow Wilson and the Fight for the League of Nations* (Cambridge: Cambridge University Press, 2001); Zara Steiner, *The Lights That Failed: European International History, 1919–1933* (New York: Oxford University Press, 2005); Susan Pedersen, *The Guardians: The League of Nations and the Crisis of Empire* (New York: Oxford University Press, 2015); William Mulligan, *The Great War for Peace* (New Haven: Yale University Press, 2014); and Robert Gerwath, ed., *The Greater War, 1912–1923* (New York: Oxford University Press, 2017) are well worth reading for background and context.

Good biographies of the key leaders are surprisingly rare, but they include John Milton Cooper, *Woodrow Wilson* (New York: Vintage, 2001); A. Scott Berg, *Wilson* (New York: Berkley, 2014); Frederick Palmer, *Bliss, Peacemaker* (New York: Dodd, Mead, 1934); John Grigg, *Lloyd George: War Leader* (London: Allen Lane, 2002); and Jean-Jacques Becker, *Clemenceau: Chef de Guerre* (Paris: Armand Colin, 2012).

Insightful memoirs include Harold Nicolson, *Peacemaking, 1919* (Boston: Houghton Mifflin, 1933); James Headlam-Morley, *A Memoir of the Paris Peace Conference* (London: Methuen, 1972); and David Lloyd George's secretary and mistress Frances Stevenson, *Lloyd George: A Diary* (New York: Harper and Row, 1971).

Index

Index